carried by a *feather*

Joan Hyams Schmitz

Copyright © 2022 Joan Hyams Schmitz.

All rights reserved. This book is protected by copyright. No part of this book may be reproduced or transmitted in any form or by any means, including as photocopies or scanned-in or other electronic copies, or utilized by any information storage and retrieval system without written permission from the copyright owner.

Printed in the United States of America.

ISBN: 978-1-7332395-0-9(paperback)

For Alan and Mark

Contents

Prelude ix

PART 1: A FAMILY IS FORMED

Chapter 1   Late Bloomers 3
Chapter 2   A Son 9
Chapter 3   Cancer, Cancer, Diabetes 13
Chapter 4   Single, White Female 21
Chapter 5   The Old Soul 27

PART 2: QUADRUPLE QUAGMIRE

Chapter 6   Boys Will Be Boys 39
Chapter 7   Birds of Pray 47
Chapter 8   The Unthinkable 51
Chapter 9   Why? 57

PART 3: THE DIVINE WITHIN AND AROUND US

Chapter 10   A Segue into Secularism 71
Chapter 11   Religion of Joan 79
Chapter 12   Signs and Symbols 89
Chapter 13   A Medium with a Large Message 101

PART 4: THE TIGGER EFFECT

Chapter 14 Resilience 111
Chapter 15 The Club 119

PART 5: THERE'S NOTHING WRONG WITH WRITING

Chapter 16 Mark, My Words 127
Chapter 17 What Might Have Been 147
Chapter 18 We Three 153

After 159
Bibliography 165
Joan's Library 167
Acknowledgements 171
Author Bio 175

*In three words, I can sum up everything
I've learned about life: It goes on.*

—Robert Frost

Prelude

You were born with wings. Why prefer to crawl through life?

—Rumi

"I can't believe you are vertical."

These words were spoken to me during a conversation with an acquaintance at a party after sharing my most recent tale of tragedy. This wasn't the first time someone had made special note of my upright status after hearing about the latest and by far the worst, most extreme test of my will. I attribute my ability to stand in the face of adversity to a trait that resides within all humans—resilience. How does one dial up our innate ability to adapt to or bounce back from life's difficult experiences? For me, the answer was found in part within soulful messages delivered by a few feathered friends.

Birds have been used as symbols since ancient times. They're the only earthly creatures that spend a vast majority of their time closest to the heavens. As they soar above and around us with their aerial view of the world, they have the ability to motivate and inspire us to rise above our human concerns. They often travel in flocks or congregations, and their gift of song can rival that of any gospel choir. Birds are our winged teachers or celestial messengers from another realm, and they often share this assignment with angels. According to Whitney Hopler, "Birds and angels share a bond because both symbolize the beauty of spiritual growth."

I experienced a spiritual growth spurt during my third decade of life just prior to the unfolding of several life-changing events that would forever alter the trajectory of my course. My teeny-tiny family—father, mother, and son—embarked on a journey of epic proportions, not one for the fainthearted. In numerology, the number three signifies a spiritual being having a human experience, and together, Alan, Joan, and Mark did have quite the human experience. This isn't a tale steeped in religion. The bones of the story simmer in a soup of love, loss, and finding one's purpose and are seasoned with a sprinkling of spirituality. In no way are the messages contained within these pages meant to step on the toes of anyone's faith or belief system. I share our tale merely as a means of connecting and reaffirming that we all have "stuff." How we choose to come to terms with said stuff is different for everybody. Some utilize the information contained within the pages of self-help books, while others prefer the confines of a counselor's couch. We can also obtain insight and even resolution one-on-one or in small groups as individuals come together to affirm and confirm we've "been there, done that." And survived.

It's my intention to share the information and insights I gained as I made some sort of sense of the unfathomable and surreal. I believe we all are gifted with our own reservoir of resilience and we have the ability to tap into and fill up our tank as we travel this thing called life. This road can be narrow, rocky, and winding, making it somewhat treacherous, and it's often littered with holes designed to swallow one up should your focus be diverted for even a nanosecond. No worries. This solo, thought-provoking, cross-country trek can be less a "highway to hell" and more of a path to enlightenment. And at the end of this road, as you stand and stretch your stiff, achy legs while inhaling a deep, cleansing breath of fresh air, you'll know you have arrived at your destination: the intersection of peace and acceptance.

If you ever find yourself feeling alone and even a bit frightened at the enormity of your journey, pull over to the side, cut the engine, and glance up into the vast, never-ending landscape that is the sky. I am certain you'll find one or two winged creatures flitting about, as your feathered friends are never far from sight. And they always carry a message of hope. Emily Dickinson captured this in her poem "Hope is the thing with feathers":

> Hope is the thing with feathers
> That perches in the soul,
> And sings the tune without the words,
> And never stops at all,
> And sweetest in the gale is heard;
> And sore must be the storm
> That could abash the little bird
> That kept so many warm.
> I've heard it in the chillest land,
> And on the strangest sea;
> Yet, never, in extremity,
> It asked a crumb of me.

Part 1

A Family Is Formed

A family is a little world created by love.

—Unknown

chapter 1
Late Bloomers

Marriages are made in heaven and consummated on Earth.

—John Lyly

Shadchan. What an odd word. It's the Hebrew word for "matchmaker." And I had one. I was a retail buyer for a chain of specialty stores based in Texas. Many of the vendors I conducted business with happened to be Jewish, and one such colleague was Mindee. On one of my frequent buying trips to New York City, Mindee invited me to dinner, which also included a third party, her current boyfriend, Elliot. During the course of the evening, I shared that I was single and would be relocating from Dallas to Houston, the result of a merger between my current company, Bealls, and another retailer, Palais Royal. Elliot, the consummate shadchan, told me about his unmarried cousin Alan, who lived and worked in Houston.

We wrapped up dinner and said our goodbyes, then I hailed a cab for the brief ride to my hotel. After I reached my room, I cleaned up, changed into PJ's, and settled down in front of the TV. Not long after, the nightstand phone rang. I picked it up and heard the voice of Houston Alan for the first time. Elliot had called him after we parted ways, and Alan wasted no time in reaching out. We spoke briefly that evening, and before hanging up, I provided him with my home number. Since this was before texting and email, our blossoming friendship evolved via long-distance phone conversations. We didn't meet in person until about three months later, so neither of us knew what the other looked like. At one point, I mailed Alan a wallet-sized photo of my sister and I that had been a recent Christmas gift for our parents. I included a little note that said, "I'm the one on the right. If you prefer the one on the left, I know where she lives."

The merger between the two retailers had been completed in the spring of 1990; however, I had chosen not to make the move. Instead, I resigned my position as buyer, remained in the Dallas area, and looked for work. My job search had been unsuccessful up until this point, yet I was reluctant to pull up roots and head south. I'd been living in North Texas for ten years and generally liked the area. I knew Houston to be more humid, more congested, and, in my opinion, less attractive than its sister city, Dallas. With that in mind, I felt the need to meet Alan face-to-face and decide whether or not he had potential as more than just a phone friend. In May of that year, I planned a weekend trip to Houston and agreed to meet Alan at his apartment. Unbeknownst to him, I'd arranged a contingency plan with a friend as an "out" should his looks not match the voice and personality I'd come to know and had grown fond of over the past few months. I was never forced to enact my plan B, as one could say there was "like" at first sight. Alan was kind, gentle, warm, and engaging, and he shared my love of conversation and reading. He was a down-to-earth homebody who was egoless and nonmaterialistic. He had a soft spot for the underdog or the downtrodden, and although he didn't have much, he would have given anyone the shirt off of his back. To put it simply, Alan was a good person.

After months of fruitless job hunting, I ended up moving to Houston and was rehired as a buyer within the newly formed company. The move enabled Alan and me to spend more time together, which contributed to our growing bond, and it became more and more obvious we were the poster couple for "opposites attract." He was ten years my elder and an introverted, intellectual loner of Russian descent. Alan was the epitome of "tall, dark, and handsome," though his height at five feet, nine inches was more average than tall. He never judged a person based on their looks, appearance, or status and, therefore, wasn't very concerned with his own. He would've never thought to send me a photo of himself prior to meeting, as this would have, in his mind, suggested some sort of vanity. His favorite attire was a pair of Wrangler jeans, a white Hanes T-shirt, and work boots. As a buyer of men's apparel, I preferred my man be more *properly* attired. I used my employee discount to update Alan's wardrobe with polo shirts, khaki pants, and more appropriate footwear—nothing formal, fancy, or expensive, just clothing that made him more presentable and accentuated his lean, model-like physique. He used to say I was the only person who got dressed up to go grocery shopping—a blasphemous exaggeration!

Alan navigated life on his own terms and schedule. He never wore a watch and was rather oblivious to time, which resulted in many tardy arrivals to work and other engagements. He stumbled through life in a sort of foggy, scatterbrained manner, which meant he often misplaced items, namely his car keys. This endearing character trait resulted in my nicknaming him the "Absentminded Professor." As his meticulously organized significant other, I often wondered how much of Alan's lifetime was spent looking for things. To me, his self-induced scavenger hunts appeared as extreme wasters of time. With that said, Alan rarely succumbed to stress, as his laid-back personality didn't subscribe to external or internal pressure. His passive approach to life was so prevalent I used to joke that I often had to place my hand under his nose or watch the rise and fall of his chest to ensure he was still breathing.

I'm an extrovert, more street smart than book smart, a people person, and a stubborn, stoic German. It's these Teutonic roots that define much of my existence, and I'm fairly certain I qualify as a type A personality. I am punctual, driven, focused, and always moving. I sum up my life with these five words: "It's exhausting to be Joan." I often poked fun at Alan's turtle-paced lifestyle, and he would come right back and tell me I could benefit from learning to sit down and relax. Touché!

Our relationship flourished despite our polar-opposite personalities, and we eventually purchased a home in suburban Houston. Our newly merged life consisted of work and making improvements to the house. Alan worked six days a week as co-owner of a small business. He'd obtained a bachelor's degree in history many years earlier with the intention of becoming a teacher. However, upon returning to his home state of New York after graduation, Alan found work with Good Humor, a familiar and popular name in the ice cream business. It was there he met his future business partner, Vinnie. They relocated to Houston and opened a frozen milk business, aptly named Texas Ice Cream.

Neither of us cared much about a conventional pairing that included marriage, kids, a minivan, and such. This lackadaisical lifestyle lasted for about three years until my sister announced she was pregnant with her first child. The fact that my young sis moved through life and adulthood in a more natural order than I did triggered my motherly instinct. This had little to do with sibling rivalry and much to do with a ticking biological clock. I had just turned thirty-four, and Alan neared forty-four. Perhaps it was time to consider a more conventional way of life. Thus began a conversation about marriage and commitment that led to a wedding.

After much planning and consideration of our separate religious upbringings—he being Jewish and me being Catholic—Alan and I were married in July 1995 in a Reform synagogue. After honeymooning in California, we began our life as husband and wife, the German and the Jew. With the clock still tick-tocking away, our thoughts turned to enlarging our family. Not ones to rush into anything, we chose to add to our newly formed nucleus with a canine instead of a human. Fritz the Rottweiler would become our first "child." Two years would pass before we considered a human addition to our home. When that time came, getting pregnant would prove to be rather easy for two aging adults; however, much greater challenges lurked in our future.

chapter 2
A Son

Babies are bits of stardust, blown from the hand of God.

—Barreto

In the early 1990s, I left the retail profession for good. A longtime devotee of health and wellness, I decided to focus my work life on helping others achieve their goals to get fit. I obtained certifications in personal training and as an aerobics instructor. Houston, the fourth largest city in the United States, was at the time a mecca in the business of energy, which included oil and gas. Many of the large, successful, financially stable companies in the area offered fitness and wellness programs for their employees. I secured a position within the corporate fitness world as a fitness specialist, where I helped maintain the fitness center, worked with members on the proper usage of the cardio and strength training equipment, and taught aerobic and weight lifting classes. I'd been working at Williams, Inc., for over a year when I became pregnant. I continued with my usual duties, including group fitness instruction. During a lunchtime class early in my eighth month of pregnancy, I received a sign that Alan and I would most likely become parents sooner than my obstetrician's calculations had indicated.

Near the end of class, I felt a trickle of wet I knew wasn't sweat. Since I'm not one to walk away from something before finishing it, I completed the class and then contacted my physician, where I was instructed to head to the hospital to be checked out. Naively thinking this was all much ado about nothing, I drove myself there, leaving a bag of clothing and other items behind, certain I'd be back in time to finish my shift and collect my things. An examination revealed my water had broken. I was considered to be in premature labor, thus requiring round-the-clock monitoring.

I didn't deliver a baby that day or the day after, as my cervix refused to dilate. During one of my frequent pelvic checks for progress, the baby's heartbeat was briefly lost on the monitor. Though this proved to be a minor and harmless blip on the radar, my obstetrician decided there was no need to prolong the inevitable. I was prepped for a C-section. Minutes later, Mark Johann Hyams made his entrance into the world four weeks early on February 5, 1998. Our bundle of boy was small yet pink and vital. His Apgar score was a 9.9 on a scale of 10, indicating he was healthy despite his premature appearance. He did not, however, avoid a stay in the NICU, as he required feeding assistance. He spent one day in the critical care side and was then transferred to the step-down unit, a place where he was kept warm and cozy, snoozing in a prone position on a bed of sheepskin warmed by lights. I guess the Sudden Infant Death Syndrome (SIDS) protocol that is drilled into new parents doesn't apply in a hospital setting where the infants are monitored day and night. No sleeping on their backs for these spoiled and closely guarded newbies.

Mark remained in the hospital for one week following my discharge. Alan and I made the trek to the hospital at least twice a day for feedings. When we arrived, we often found Mark in a papoose strapped to one of the nurses as she tended to the other infants. Mark had become a favorite of the staff for some unknown reason. But who cared about the reason? Our baby was being coddled and cuddled by an attentive and highly trained nursing staff during our absence. After gaining the obligatory amount of weight, Mark was discharged on Valentine's Day. I can't think of a more fitting date to bring home the newest addition of love to a family.

We spent the next days and weeks settling into life as new parents. Our time and energy were focused on feeding, burping, diapering, snuggling, and marveling at our miracle. I was given the precious gift of staying home with Mark for three months before returning to work in a part-time capacity. It was around then that life began to unravel.

chapter 3
Cancer, Cancer, Diabetes

Dear Cancer, I hope one day you're just a zodiac sign.
—Curiano.com

In May 1998, just three months after the birth of our son, Alan began experiencing back pain. This chronic ache wasn't debilitating enough to keep him from work but was more of a nuisance that refused to go away. He lived with this unexplained yet manageable pain for over two months before deciding to have it checked out, first with a visit to a chiropractor and then a follow-up with a physician. Scans revealed Alan's nagging back pain was far more serious than a strain of his muscles or some other benign issue. A biopsy was performed, and the results indicated a rare and often fatal form of cancer—poorly differentiated carcinoma of unknown primary. The last two words proved to be far more fear inducing than the actual c-word itself, as this meant a specific cell type couldn't be identified. Doctors were unable to determine the origin of the disease. Had this cancerous invasion begun in the lung, colon, pancreas, or brain? Pinpointing the cell type aids considerably in mapping out a specific and proven course of treatment. And if this wasn't bad enough, the scans also revealed metastasis. Alan's slow-growing, secret invader had set up camp at other sites within his body, including his stomach, chest, and adrenal gland. Metastasis can reduce one's chances of survival by 50 percent.

The medical personnel involved with Alan's case—we obtained two opinions—had to make an educated guess as to the origin of this intruder and then make a determination as to the best course of treatment. Alan felt like a caged lab rat, an unwilling test specimen in cancer research. He simply had no other choice than to accept their hypothesis and prepare for the fight of his life.

Alan, an otherwise healthy male, underwent chemotherapy and radiation and sought out holistic methods of treatment as well. The usual prognosis for this type of cancer is three to six months. Alan was able to beat those odds and extend his survival to just over three years. He proved that having a will to live, namely in the form of wanting to experience the joys of fatherhood, can add quality time to your life despite what doctors or studies suggest.

Alan passed away in the wee hours of Monday, September 10, 2001, two months shy of his fifty-first birthday. He left us one day before the horrific, terroristic events of September 11, a date that forever altered the landscape and serenity of our country. To this day, I'm unaware of much of the tragedy that took place early on that Tuesday morning, as I refused to partake in the round-the-clock coverage. I couldn't bear to strap on the grief and suffering of so many when my own family's hopes and dreams had also crashed and burned with Alan's passing. I also recall I felt a bit guilty about having the knowledge my spouse was nearing the end of his life, which offered some semblance of mental preparation, though one is never fully prepared to lose a loved one. I felt so much sadness, compassion, and empathy for the thousands who sent their family members, friends, and acquaintances off to work that day or bid them farewell as they boarded planes bound for some predetermined destination, only to learn they would never again return home. I also remember feeling somewhat cheated at having survived three grueling years of life with cancer, only to learn that we, the United States of America, had risen to the top of a most-hated list, endangering the existence and livelihood of an entire nation. The dark cloud of cancer that had hovered over my family had now been replaced by a cloak of terror donned by millions.

Less than two months after Alan's passing, I sold our home in Houston and relocated my family—mother, child, and canine—to the town of my birth, Cincinnati, Ohio. This tribe of three began to establish a new normal in our cozy, ranch-style, suburban home. Mark attended preschool, and I found work. We now lived in close proximity to my mother, sister, brother-in-law, and my two nephews. Looking back some time later, I realized I'd dismissed feelings of anger and grief, emotions that had most likely surfaced at the time of Alan's diagnosis and had become more intense with his passing. I also came to learn that grief must be dealt with and the best way to do this is head on. There's no sidestepping or maneuvering around it. The way to come to some sort of peace with grief is by going *through* it. Should you decide to postpone or neglect grief, it will patiently sit in a corner and wait. And that's exactly what grief did for me. It. Waited. I'd come to pay a heavy price for believing I could bury my thoughts and feelings along with Alan on the grassy hill of a cemetery.

In June 2003, twenty-one months after Alan's passing, I experienced allergy-like congestion accompanied by a crippling, come-out-of-nowhere fatigue that climaxed days later with an unexplained, nonstop nosebleed. An evening trip to the ER resulted in a battery of tests designed to determine the cause of my leaky nose. A bone marrow biopsy performed the following morning confirmed that cancer had once again found my family. This time it was my turn.

I was diagnosed with a rare form of acute myeloid leukemia, of which there are several subtypes. My subtype is referred to as acute promyelocytic leukemia or M3. If detected early like mine was, it has an extremely high rate of cure.

One of the first things my oncologist said to me was, "You have the good leukemia." My immediate thought upon hearing his comment was, "Isn't that an oxymoron?" How does one say "good" and "leukemia" in the same sentence? Nevertheless, unlike Alan's shot-in-the dark treatment, my cancer had a specific and proven plan of action, which included four rounds of intravenous chemotherapy followed by two years of maintenance chemo administered in pill form. If one completes this regimen with no return of those nasty blast cells, the patient is considered cured.

In August 2005, two months shy of my cure date, I began planning a thank-you celebration. I intended to invite the village of people who had helped Mark and me during this difficult and challenging time. However, life was about to take yet another turn. There would be no time or inclination to celebrate at all.

Just days into August 2005, Mark experienced bouts of extreme thirst. In response, he gulped down vast amounts of fluid, which resulted in frequent trips to the bathroom. I'm somewhat medically savvy and had a pretty good idea what these symptoms might indicate, but I allowed myself a few days of denial in the hope that another life-threatening illness hadn't found its way into our lives. This was not to be. On a warm, sunny, summer day, halfway through his seventh year of life, Mark was diagnosed with type 1 diabetes, formerly known as juvenile diabetes. This currently incurable, life-threatening disease is one of many listed under the heading of "autoimmune," where the body attacks itself for reasons unknown. In Mark's case, his pancreas was the target of this silent invasion, which destroyed his insulin-producing beta cells. Insulin is a hormone necessary to convert sugar/glucose, starches, and other food into energy necessary for life. Mark began a daily regimen of finger sticks, insulin shots, carb counting, and numerous visits to a local diabetes clinic for checkups.

The initial days and weeks after Mark's diagnosis were consumed with learning the ins and outs of diabetes care, which is tedious and somewhat regimented yet is in no way an exact science. There's a fair amount of room for error, such as mistakes in insulin doses, carb counting, or exercise, which can result in extreme low or high blood sugars that can become immediately life-threatening. Life with diabetes can be a constant "walking on eggshells" kind of existence, always tiptoeing around the numbers on a blood sugar meter. Mark could no longer grab a snack from the pantry or fridge or sit down to a meal without first checking his blood sugar, adding up the amount of carbohydrates he intended to consume, dialing up the proper amount of insulin to cover the carbs, and then injecting himself. He had to carry a meter, insulin pen, supplies, and sugar on him wherever he went, as he could never stray far from these life-saving instruments. Simply put, Mark was once again robbed of a normal existence.

In the months and even years following Mark's diabetes diagnosis, I spent time reflecting on the events that occurred between 1998 and 2005, a period I refer to as our Trifecta of Trauma. I faced two of the events without the support of my spouse and co-parent. It was just me and my little boy, two humans doing their best to make the most out of a life that didn't go as planned. Or did it? Is it possible our story had been carefully crafted and scripted long ago in a distant and beautiful place? William Shakespeare says this best in a line taken from his play *As You Like It*: "All the world's a stage, and all the men and women merely players."

Over time, it became clear that the youngest cast member in our tale of three might be the wisest and is, therefore, deserving of his own backstory. However, before I can intimately acquaint you with my son, Mark, I must first introduce you to another guy.

chapter 4
Single, White Female

*If we meet offline and you look nothing like your
pics, you're buying me drinks until you do.*

—www.zackkingkhan.net

In the span of seven years, my family was thrust into a tailspin of epic proportions that left no one unscathed. Events had occurred in such a rapid-fire progression it was impossible to wrap my head around all that had transpired. Cancer had stalked us, kidnapped the patriarch of our nucleus, and invaded my body, forever causing me to teeter on the fine line between survivor and patient. And diabetes not only deprived Mark of his right to a healthy body, but it also knocked me right off of my feet. Literally. In the days, weeks, and months following Mark's diagnosis, I recall feeling much like a boxer on the receiving end of a knockout punch. As the diabetic blow was dealt, I was toppled to the mat, facedown, battered and bruised in a semiconscious state while the referee stood over me counting—one, two, three. I never disclosed my deep-rooted fear, concern, and depression-like sadness to Mark as we incorporated diabetes into our daily life. Only when he was away at school or otherwise occupied did I allow myself the time to weep in body-wracking sobs, grieving my child's loss of health and the always looming threat that this disease could snatch him from me.

I ever so slowly began to come to terms with the Trifecta of Trauma that had invaded the tranquility of our home and existence. I never entertained the idea of dating or remarriage, as I couldn't conceive of inviting anyone into our lives where danger seemed to lurk behind darkened doors. Also, getting acquainted with a potential mate requires copious amounts of time and energy. I was more intent on making Mark the focus of my days and nights, as childhood is but a brief blip on the radar of life. And where was I supposed to meet this future mate? I rarely went out and was surrounded by couples within my suburban existence.

I blew out fifty candles not long after Mark made the official transition into his teen years. As a side note, it's not a good idea for a mother to enter menopause around the same time a child enters puberty. All of those hormones in flux can lead to an extremely harried existence, which may or may not include many heated interactions. And that "heat" is often generated via a hot flash. By this time, Alan had been gone for over nine years. I looked ahead to a time in the not-so-distant future when Mark would most likely head off to college, leaving me alone in a semi-empty nest. Well, almost alone. We now shared our home with a lovable Labrador retriever, Miss Lexi Lou, our rescue canine and also my stalker. At the urging of friends and coworkers, I entertained the idea of looking for love on the internet via online dating sites. In January 2011, I signed up for two sites with the intention of investing a minimum of one year into this process, which I believed offered it a fair chance at success. And this search wouldn't be a private or confidential endeavor. I started a blog a few years earlier where I shared posts about single parenthood, boys, books, canines, cancer, and other random musings. In an effort to stick to my plan to delve into the world of internet matchmaking, I decided to blog my way through this somewhat scary and foreign process. These posts can be found on my blog, *Joan's Jottings*, at jfh48.blog.

Every week, Monday through Saturday, I scoured my matches and made notes about the mostly divorced dads in my target age range of forty-seven to fifty-seven. It soon became obvious that I'd voluntarily jumped into a world that was less about finding a soulmate and more about finding a bed mate. The things aged men wrote in their online bios became fodder for my posts. With that said, I never divulged names, nor were my summaries designed to make fun of or inflict hurt upon anyone. I shared the ridiculous, juvenile, frat-boy, sexually infused words and photos many men posted in an effort to attract women. Here is one example that requires no explanation. Every member used a name or handle to identify their page. This might be a clever phrase or nickname or a combination of letters and numbers. There were a select group of male love-seekers who included the number "69" as part of their title. Really? I often wondered if Mr. 69 also carried a bottle of Viagra or Cialis on his person in an effort to live up to his Hugh Hefner alter ego. I posted my weekly recap every Sunday and soon developed a loyal following of mostly happily married females. My readers were provided a glimpse into what single life looks like in the twenty-first century, which they enjoyed from the safety of their suburban sofas.

My internet dating sites did introduce me to a few men who I agreed to meet in person. I had lunch dates with two of them where, minutes into the meal, I detected an error in the dating site algorithm. We were not a match! I politely indulged in conversation until an appropriate time presented itself as an escape. I met a third match for coffee and conversation. We enjoyed each other's company, so I agreed to accompany him to a local event a few days later. It was during this time I began to find him somewhat arrogant and one of many not looking for a long-term relationship but more of a one-night stand. There was no third date.

I stuck to my commitment as the months ticked by until September rolled into October. After nine months and forty-six posts, I canceled my subscriptions and officially signed off as Joan, the online dating blogger. I'd had enough. I never did have much faith in this process, as I believe love has a way of finding you if you're open to receiving it. Looking for love makes about as much sense as looking for a needle in a haystack. I believe it's better to cruise through life with the top down and zero expectations and to remain open to what or whom you might pick up along the way. And for the record, I prefer to travel on Route 66, not Route 69!

My "lookin' for love" philosophy proved to be true just days after logging off when I met a man at a local charity event, where it should be noted I was not on the hunt for love. This was no chance encounter, as there were close to four thousand people in attendance in the expansive convention center venue. Guy Schmitz is four years my junior and also a member of the widows club, having lost his wife to heart-related issues. He'd been single-parenting his only child for fourteen months when we met. We began our courtship in the days immediately following our initial, divinely arranged meeting. We lived about thirty miles from one another, so we mostly saw each other on weekends. On weekday evenings, we checked in via phone, and these conversations often lasted for hours. On Sundays, the four of us often spent the day together, going to some event or enjoying a meal. These gatherings provided time for us to become acquainted with one another and a way to begin the blending of our families. We married three years later, combining households just as Guy's daughter headed off to college and Mark entered his junior year of high school.

I often describe Guy as one of the best humans I've ever met. Period. He's a loving and devoted son, husband, father, brother, uncle, and friend, and he is hardworking, loyal, and fun. He's an outgoing extrovert with an infectious zest for life. His quick wit often makes him the life of any party or gathering. We often engage in a certain kind of back-and-forth banter that for any outsider might sound like an argument. It's all in jest and a way for us to poke fun at each other's quirks and idiosyncrasies. Guy's a thoughtful romantic—think cards, flowers, gifts, and my first horse carriage ride. He's been my biggest cheerleader and supporter, especially in regard to my writing. He's not only my spouse but also my best friend. He arrived in our life with precision timing as Mark navigated his way through the tests and trials of his teenage years. Guy provided Mark with positive male mentoring that had been mostly absent in the years since Alan's passing. They became buddies, sharing a yearning for Mexican food and pizza as well as for Star Wars and old movies. And Guy was no "step" father. I've always disliked the term "step" parent, as I believe it has a somewhat negative connotation, such as in "Cinderella" and similar tales. A former coworker introduced me to the term "bonus" parent, a word that more accurately describes what Guy provided Mark. He was the extra special that had been missing in the life of a boy so wrought with challenges and heartbreak.

chapter 5
The Old Soul

Quiet people have the loudest minds.
—Stephen Hawking

Mark's arrival in this lifetime might have been premature from a medical standpoint; however, looking back, I'm convinced he arrived here at a divinely planned, precise, and perfect moment on that February afternoon in Houston, Texas. He'd come to this lifetime, into the arms of his meticulously selected family of origin, with a suitcase full of wisdom acquired over many, many prior visits to Earth. My boy was no boy in the spiritual sense. But I'm getting ahead of myself.

I realized very early on that Mark was unique. He was a fairly easy baby, spending the majority of his time eating, cooing, and messing diapers. Did you happen to notice how I didn't include sleeping in my description of a typical day in the life of young Mark Hyams? As a new mother, I assumed infants spent the majority of their time in slumber, as ample rest seemed necessary to support the rapid speed at which their tiny minds and bodies developed. For the first five months, Mark rarely slept. He spent most of his days and nights wide awake, soaking up the sights and sounds of his new world. I attribute some of this to the spoiling he received in the NICU, where he passed most of his time on his belly, snuggled in a sheepskin blanket. At home, I laid him down to sleep on his back according to SIDS protocol or propped him up in a vibrating seat I hoped would lull him into some state of rest. Neither of these situations provided adequate periods of slumber. Mark preferred to obtain his rest in catnap sequences throughout the day, nodding off like an old man lulled into sleep by quiet and perhaps boredom. It seems possible Mark believed if he drifted off for even a few hours at a time, something would be missed, and he was having none of that! Of course, Mark's manic refusal to sleep also meant I rarely slept, the details of which I can share in a future book titled *Sleep Deprivation: One Mother's Path to Insanity*.

As Mark morphed from infant to toddler, it became increasingly apparent he was a shy, quiet child. He definitely had inherited his father's introverted personality. Mark lived his life with a fine-tuned focus and awareness. He was keenly observant and cognizant of everything around him, filing the ordinary and routine events of a day into his highly organized and deep-thinking mind. He'd often make note of something that had occurred, ponder it for a while, and later blurt out some mature and insightful summation of said event.

As the days and months of his infancy passed, Mark checked off developmental milestones in a fashion considered early for boys. He conquered walking by the age of ten months and, for the most part, took control of his own potty training once he was provided with instructions and a portable, pint-sized john. Like most kids, he slowly built a vocabulary—a word here, a word there. However, once his right-brain neurons began firing with greater frequency and speed, more and more terms were added to his inner dictionary. He literally spewed sentences, and these weren't "See Dick run" phrases. Mark communicated as if a bearded, wise, cane-carrying, Jewish man of rabbinical proportions had taken over his voice. I remember with distinct clarity an example of such an occurrence when then three-year-old Mark met me at the back door as I arrived home from an appointment with an orthopedic surgeon.

At this particular juncture, Alan had been living his life-with-cancer journey for three years. His end was nearing, though we weren't privy to how little time he had remaining. Mark was not yet old enough to fully grasp or understand the critical nature of Alan's long-fought battle, but his intuitive and introspective mind had to be playing a toddler version of connect the dots. He knew his once vibrant and active father no longer went to work and spent most of his days propped up in bed. The cancer, which now spread like a rumor mill in a small town, had chosen bone as its newest place of residence, preferring the bones in his legs and hips. This metastasis now induced pain as well as marked interference with Alan's ability to walk. He relied on crutches or a walker to get back and forth from the bed to the bathroom, and we had a wheelchair for times he wanted to leave the confines of the bedroom and engage with us in other parts of our home. Alan's physical decline was obvious, especially in the eyes of a young boy. I tried to keep certain conversations confidential and private, but there had to be times when Mark's immature ears picked up on words that were unfamiliar and had a certain tone of gloom and doom—cancer, treatments, doctors, X-rays, bedridden, and, ultimately, hospice.

And so on that August afternoon when I informed Mark I was leaving for an appointment with a doctor, who knows what kind of large and scary thoughts entered the mind of my young yet highly perceptive boy? When I returned, Mark met me at the back door with a blunt and direct question: "So what did the doctor say?" Somewhere deep within the hidden recesses of his mind, Mark needed to be the first one to determine if my appointment with a doctor might result in his mother and only full-time caregiver also becoming incapacitated and unable to care for him, his dad, and the dog. This brief interaction got me thinking about the possibility that I was living with a boy wise beyond his years.

After Alan passed away and the responsibility for Mark's care and upbringing fell solely in my lap, I found myself at times struggling to understand and fully grasp Mark's highly sensitive nature. A friend recommended the book *Raising Your Spirited Child: A Guide for Parents Whose Child Is More Intense, Sensitive, Perceptive, Persistent, and Energetic* by Mary Sheedy Kurcinka, which became my how-to manual for living with and raising my very own "spirited" child. With stunning accuracy, Ms. Kurcinka described Mark's God-given personality and offered copious amounts of advice on how best to parent this type of child, my boy who marched to a different drummer. I read and reread portions of this book countless times from Mark's toddlerhood into his school-age years.

Once Mark entered preschool, kindergarten, and beyond, I continued to gain insight into his personality and how he interacted with the world outside the comfort and safety of our home. When Mark and his fellow students gathered together on the classroom floor for some sort of group lesson, he always chose to sit alone outside the circle. I don't know if Mark's teachers ever attempted to coax him into joining the group; however, his kindergarten teacher did her best to lure him out of his shell. Mark never played with anyone during recess, choosing instead to stand alone for the entire allotted time. His teacher made several attempts to pair Mark with another shy boy. I believe this worked on rare occasions; however, more often than not, Mark chose to spend time alone. And then suddenly, three weeks before the end of the school year, Mark began engaging with the other kids on the playground. He'd finally warmed up, and he did it on his own schedule.

One time when Mark was about seven or eight, I asked him about his choice to consistently segregate himself from the class. Mark's response was blunt and to the point: "You're the one who has a problem with it. I don't." Wow! Message received. Year after year, Mark took his time warming up to his teacher and classmates. However, as he matured, this acclimation sped up. He rarely spoke in class or raised his hand in participation, but he listened intently and always completed his work, often making him a favorite of the teacher. It's possible for an attentive, quiet, well-behaved child to unknowingly don a Harry Potter cloak of invisibility, allowing them to disappear from the radar of their busy and often distracted instructor. If Mark struggled with a subject or assignment, he rarely asked for help, as this required drawing attention to himself. For example, Mark fell a bit behind with reading during first grade but was quickly brought up to speed with the help of a reading specialist.

Throughout his childhood, Mark limited his friendships to a select few, spending most of his time with one or two trusted friends. Later on, as I reflected on these relationships, it became obvious Mark mostly attracted extroverts as his playmates. Perhaps this is why most of these friendships didn't endure the test of time. As the boys grew older and began to mature, the extroverts drifted away from Mark, gravitating toward others who shared their more social and expressive personalities. Also, Mark could be a bit anal, intense, and quirky, which might have also turned off a friend or two. No harm, no foul. Mark always managed to find his way to new friendships as old ones met their natural demise.

During his years at an all-boys high school, I received further insight into Mark and his personality. Early in his sophomore year, the entire class was administered the well-known and widely used Myers-Briggs personality test. If you're unfamiliar with this test and the interpretation of its results, here's a little background information.

In the 1920s, Carl G. Jung presented his theory of personality types. The Myers-Briggs test, created in the 1940s by a mother-daughter team, was designed to take Jung's theory and make it accessible, understandable, and useful in the lives of individuals. The results of the test offer information into how people perceive and interact in the world and how this influences their decisions. There's no "best in show" among the sixteen distinctive personality types, as everyone is equal. Mark's results indicated he had a very rare personality type—ISFJ, an acronym that stands for introvert, sensate, feeler, judger. Mark was one of only two boys out of four hundred whose results indicated these particular traits. In a somewhat ironic twist, the second young man with test results suggesting ISFJ was part of Mark's social group.

As Mark and I perused his results, it became evident he was somewhat upset about the insights it provided. I think the ISFJ label caused him to feel inferior in some way, which in turn poked at his somewhat fragile self-esteem. I believe as he continued to age and mature, he no longer wanted to sit outside the circle like he'd done throughout his early school years. Like most teens, he wanted to belong and fit in, and he thought this label excluded him from the popular or more common group, most likely comprised of outgoing, outspoken extroverts.

I explained first and foremost that this evaluation was just one of many predictors of personality and shouldn't be read as black or white, as every test has room for a margin of error, therefore imparting a middle ground or area of gray. Secondly, we're all unique and individual and can't be boxed into some tidy, compact package. Humans are a combination of a lot of things, including our heritage and our environment. Furthermore, every one of us is born with certain positive attributes or strengths, and it's up to us to recognize our gifts and nurture them so we can share them with the world.

Upon further review of the literature that accompanied the Myers-Briggs results, we learned the ISFJ individual possesses many attractive and noteworthy traits, including that they are quiet, gentle, and caring.

ISFJs are slow to warm up to new people, but once they do, they're extremely loyal.

They're cautious about jumping into social situations and might resist trying new experiences, choosing to spend time with one or two close and trusted friends. These last two statements reaffirmed my long-held observation of Mark and his slow-to-warm-up nature when confronted with new people and situations. I found a quote from an unknown source that accurately sums up Mark's interactions with new people: "The funny thing about introverts is once they feel comfortable with you, they can be the funniest, most enjoyable people to be around. It's like a secret they feel comfortable sharing with you. Except the secret is their personality."

The ISFJ is considerate, respectful, and sensitive, and they tend to avoid tension and conflict. They're also unpretentious, practical, and sincere.

As the devoted and observant extroverted parent of an introverted child, I often thought about and analyzed the vast differences in our personalities and how they related to the world at large. I believed and still believe that in many ways it's easier to navigate one's way through life as an extrovert; however, I know the world desperately needs introverts and their immense contributions to schools, the workplace, and the community. Their silent observations and resulting summations significantly influence and contribute to the betterment of society as a whole.

I recently read the book *Quiet: The Power of Introverts in a World That Can't Stop Talking* by Susan Cain. Regrettably, I wasn't aware this body of work existed when Mark began high school, as it would have provided me with even greater insight into his personality, and I could have shared these insights with him as we discussed the Myers-Briggs test. And if Mark had chosen to read it, he would have gained valuable information in regard to his personality that might have enabled him to appreciate and even be thankful for his introverted gift.

I found the following statement on Quotes Central, which offers a humorous explanation of the difference between the two personality types: "Asking an introvert to open up is as rude as asking an extrovert to shut up."

I know Mark often left a favorable impression on others even as a young lad. With that said, he also possessed the stereotypical male characteristics, the ones that tend to drive women mad. These include immaturity, impulsiveness, laziness, and the inability to respond to nosy motherly inquiries with more than a grunt of one or two monosyllabic words. Oh, and smelly feet. It was with these feet that Mark often straddled two worlds—the innocent and often naive world of a growing and evolving boy and the insightful and wise world of someone far beyond their chronological age.

Part 2
Quadruple Quagmire

Tough times don't define you. They refine you.

—Unknown

chapter 6
Boys Will Be Boys

Little boys should never be sent to bed.
They always wake up a day older.

—Peter Pan

Information is indeed knowledge, especially when it comes to raising children. However, it's important to recognize we aren't living with and parenting a "personality." In my case, I was single-handedly raising a boy who would experience all of the growing pains, both physical and psychological, that are part of the human developmental process. As Mark's parent and teacher, it was up to me to nurture, encourage, and guide him and to instill in him the morals, mores, and values that would aid him in becoming a thoughtful, generous, and productive member of society.

He was expected to help around the house and abide by the rules and standards established by me. As many parents can confirm, there are times when a child will attempt to sidestep the system, bending or even breaking the rules. This occurred in our home on more occasions than I care to remember. These instances are a test of a parent's ability to stick to their guns and not surrender to a whiny toddler or tolerate the back talk of a moody teenager. And these tests can prove to be mentally and physically exhausting, especially for those of us engaged in these battles without the support and backup of a copilot. I was an army of one, the good cop and the bad cop. Mark could be stubborn and unyielding, traits he most likely inherited from me. We often bumped heads, and much of this noggin knockin' was the result of Mark's fascination and obsession with video gaming.

Like so many teenagers of Mark's generation, he spent hours upon hours on PlayStation, Xbox 360, and a gaming computer he and a friend built. I don't think there is much positive that can be said in regard to video games, as I believe they can be addicting, and they also introduce violence into the innocent minds of young players. They're a gobbler of time that otherwise could be spent with family, doing schoolwork, or engaging in some sort of sport or physical activity outdoors. The invention of the interactive gaming headset is perhaps the only positive in regard to this pastime. This device enabled Mark to game with friends without ever leaving the confines of his bedroom. Unfortunately, this time spent at home consisted of Mark holed up in his room, hidden behind a closed door. From the ages of thirteen or fourteen into young adulthood, I saw the outside of his bedroom door more than I saw his face.

During Mark's later teen years, I learned about his exposure to alcohol and marijuana. I didn't freak out when I became aware of these teenage rites of passage, as I'd done my share of experimentation with these substances. For as much as I know, Mark tried things, and he appeared to be less smart or savvy than his counterparts in handling these situations. Or perhaps he was too naive.

After completing high school, Mark chose to continue his education and was accepted to Miami University in Oxford, Ohio. Three weeks into his freshman year, Mark was caught by campus police in an underage drinking situation. He wasn't taken into custody but was driven by ambulance to the local hospital after he informed the officer he was diabetic. Guy and I learned about the incident just hours after it occurred and made the short trip to campus to speak with Mark, to check on his condition, and to learn more about his account of the evening's events. We talked about the dangers of alcohol and drugs, which can be especially perilous for a diabetic, as well as reinforced our expectation he remain focused on his studies. We also allowed Mark to lawyer up in order to get the misdemeanor charge expunged from his permanent record. Guy and I are united in our belief that humans often obtain the most growth and wisdom by making mistakes. We believed Mark listened as we counseled him, and we used the opportunity to remind him he could reach out to us day or night for *anything*. We believed Mark had learned a lesson from his encounter with law enforcement and the judicial system, so we didn't force him to come home or withdraw from the university.

Two months later, Mark and three dorm friends were caught smoking marijuana in a wooded area on campus grounds. Once again, a call was made to the attorney, which resulted in additional fees and a second court appearance. The university also required Mark to attend a day-long class on substance abuse as well as submit a letter of apology to the school, admitting he'd violated their policies. If there was any positive in all of the negative Mark chose to bring upon himself, he did attend class and maintained decent grades, although they weren't as high as they'd been in his elementary through high school years. By the end of his tumultuous freshman year, he had successfully completed thirty-three credit hours.

Mark had chosen psychology as his major and was interested in adding a minor. At the urging of his freshman English teacher, Mark considered creative writing as a possibility. He eventually scheduled a meeting with an advisor within the English department who added linguistics to what would become a growing list of considerations. Mark allowed these ideas to roll around in his head as he entered his sophomore year, where he began to feel drawn to IT as a possible choice. Mark was fond of computers and not just for gaming. Like many young people today, he'd grown up using electronic devices, which enabled him to acquire a certain amount of knowledge regarding their operating systems. He often performed upgrades to his desktop computer as well as his laptop. Mark did meet with an advisor within the Computer Science department and began to seriously consider pursuing some sort of IT minor. When the time came to schedule courses for the spring semester of his sophomore year, Mark chose Fundamentals: Programming and Problem Solving, an introductory course within the Computer Science department, as a way to test the waters. If he was able to comprehend the material and achieve a decent grade, he intended to seriously consider some sort of computer science minor.

The one thing Mark had been neglecting to do as he navigated his way through the first three semesters of college was to get involved. Not long after being accepted to the university, Mark applied for and was selected as one of only eighteen students in the newly created D.I.V.E. program, which stands for Diverse Immersion & Volunteer Experience. As an incoming freshman and member of this initiative, Mark was able to move into his dorm a few days early, where he spent time getting acquainted with staff and other students as well as being introduced to community engagement and social justice at the university level. The group also spent a day in nearby Cincinnati, completing a clean-up project.

This type of community involvement wasn't new to Mark, as he donated dozens of volunteer hours throughout his high school career, including time spent at Bethany House, a shelter for homeless women and their children. Mark and his fellow volunteers babysat the children while the mothers attended self-enrichment classes. In the summer of 2015, Mark traveled to Guatemala with ten classmates and two teacher chaperones as part of a mission trip. This contingent aided locals in building an addition to a new school that would provide education to many of the underprivileged children in the region.

It seems possible that in those first three semesters at the university a rigorous academic schedule combined with time dedicated to social endeavors prevented Mark from pursuing résumé building activities that would better serve him down the road. Guy and I had many conversations with him regarding his lack of involvement in campus activities not social in nature. In fact, early on in his fourth semester, we gave him an ultimatum—get involved with something, which included securing some sort of employment, or move home and commute to campus. Mark followed through on our directives, as he obtained part-time work just weeks into the semester. I guess we should've been more specific about the kind of work he chose, as this underage, slightly built young man became a bouncer at a local campus bar. We also learned Mark had been in contact with the local chapter of Big Brothers and Big Sisters. He'd mentioned on more than one occasion that he and a friend were interested in learning more about this organization that pairs adult men and women with youth in need of friendship and mentoring.

It was our hope that as Mark matured and found his comfort zone within the vast world life on a college campus offered, he'd become bored with some of the social antics and aspects of this life and begin to focus more on his long-range goals, which included graduation and possibly graduate school. It's my belief he was beginning to listen to the unwanted yet sage advice and edicts of his parents and was attempting to make better choices. This is largely the reason why we never enforced our ultimatum—get it together or move home. We provided him with the opportunity to learn from his mistakes and readjust his focus.

If Mark was going to be successful in following through with his goals, living his life in a way that reflected the morals and values that had been instilled in him within our home, school, and community, it was also probable that he needed to move on from some of his friends and acquaintances. Walking away from unhealthy or toxic relationships is difficult for anyone regardless of age and experience, and it can be even more difficult for a young person like Mark who spent much of his life trying to fit in. He genuinely cared about people and was especially drawn to fellow underdogs like himself. In my opinion, Mark was entangled in a few relationships that weren't healthy or beneficial for *all* parties involved. As time marched on, it became clear that Mark's inexperience, immaturity, naivete, procrastination, and somewhat fragile self-esteem interfered with his ability to make good choices.

Like many young people, Mark tested the waters of independence that life on a college campus provides. There are tons of tests within the confines of a university, and many of them come from outside the classroom. According to a dean of students at Miami University, "The ages between eighteen and twenty-two are ones of extreme exploration and experimentation." I believe Mark was exploring and experimenting as many young adults do, so his somewhat reckless behavior and crappy choices weren't uncommon or out of the ordinary. The million-dollar question, however, remained hanging in the balance: Was he learning from his mistakes? It's okay to make mistakes, but it's not okay to keep repeating the same ones over and over again. In my opinion, repeated mistakes are indicative of a failure to learn and change. Author Phyllis Theroux sums it up this way: "Mistakes are the *usual* bridge between inexperience and wisdom." Would Mark learn from his repeated transgressions and make the changes necessary for him to fulfill his goals as well as live his life according to the moral code that had been instilled in him since birth?

chapter 7
Birds of Pray

In order to see birds, it is necessary to become part of the silence.

—Robert Lynd

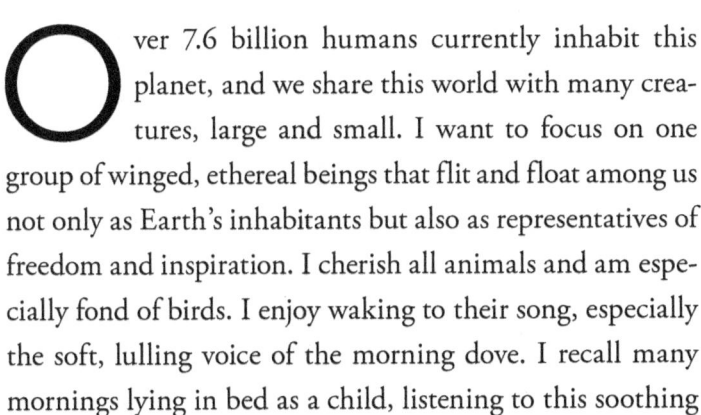

Over 7.6 billion humans currently inhabit this planet, and we share this world with many creatures, large and small. I want to focus on one group of winged, ethereal beings that flit and float among us not only as Earth's inhabitants but also as representatives of freedom and inspiration. I cherish all animals and am especially fond of birds. I enjoy waking to their song, especially the soft, lulling voice of the morning dove. I recall many mornings lying in bed as a child, listening to this soothing dove music. Birds are considered messengers, often serving as bridges between two worlds. Chris Welch sums up their

existence in this way: "Birds have long thought to be associated with otherworldly powers—not other planetary but otherworldly, as in the spirit world."

I've had numerous encounters with birds and believe these interactions aren't the result of chance or accident. In 2016, Guy and I had not one but two incidences where a bird gained entrance into our home. The first visit occurred one evening as the doorbell rang, informing us a neighbor couple had stopped by. As we opened the door, a sparrow entered our home as well. This unexpected guest flew around the house, confused and somewhat disoriented. Within a short span of time, the bird headed toward the back of the house, where it landed on a bedroom lamp. A towel was placed over the entire light fixture, capturing this tiny, frightened creature. The lamp and bird were carried outside, where the uninvited visitor was set free. I recall our neighbor saying something along the lines of "A bird in the home means something bad is going to happen," which I brushed off and forgot about.

A few months later, we had the flooring replaced in our home. The crew worked daily for about a week, ripping up the old carpet and baseboards and installing hardwood flooring. Our garage was command central for this project. The men made frequent trips outside, where the garage door remained open while they worked. Late one morning, a small bird, most likely another sparrow, flew into the garage and couldn't find its way out. After spending several minutes attempting to free the frightened creature, I went inside, booted up the computer, and searched for information. I learned if a bird finds its way into an enclosed space, it can become trapped and unable to locate an exit, which in this case was a large, wide-open garage door. It will flit and flutter around and around, often to the point of exhaustion and even death. After the crew left for the day, Guy and I used rakes and a broom to gently guide the bird from the ceiling to a lower elevation, resulting in its freedom. Many people leave their garage doors open for hours at a time when performing yardwork or another project and are never privy to such an experience with a bird. I considered this second avian encounter somewhat strange and mysterious. But once again, I tossed it into the recesses of my mind and let it go.

Were our two encounters with birds random occurrences? Many cultures have long-held superstitions or old wives' tales that reference the rare phenomenon of a bird entering a home via a door or window. They consider it an omen for someone in the household. And lest you think the word *omen* only implies something negative, think again. *Merriam-Webster* defines an omen as an "occurrence or phenomenon." Notice words of judgment, such as "good" or "bad," aren't used. *Wikipedia* describes it in this way: "A phenomenon that is believed to foretell the future, often signifying the advent of change. People in ancient times believed that omens brought a divine message from their gods." I don't think we should place judgment on messages delivered by birds. They're merely relaying information between here and there. They are spiritual mail carriers just doing their job.

chapter 8
The Unthinkable

There are moments that mark your life, moments
when you realize nothing will ever be the same.
And time is divided into two parts,
before this and after this.

—Unknown

The invention of the cell phone has been a game changer in the manner in which we conduct our lives. As with most things, there are positive and negative aspects associated with these devices. For me, the cell phone provided a means to instantly connect with my son during times of separation. Mark received his first phone when he was in sixth grade, providing him with 24/7 access to friends, the internet, a camera, and a video recorder.

There were occasions where I had to remind him the main reason he'd been gifted with a phone was to keep in contact with me. Period. This meant that when I called or texted, I expected to receive some sort of reply within a reasonable amount of time.

Mark began his fourth semester at Miami University in late January 2018. We permitted him to return to campus and his dorm, though certain expectations as far as his grades and school involvement had now been put into place. We were forced to once again remind him of these expectations in late February, as we learned of yet another instance where he'd broken university rules. The cord that tethered him between our home (dependence) and college life (independence) had been stretched to its limit. Mark was literally at the end of his rope as far as we were concerned.

In the late afternoon of Wednesday, March 7, I began texting Mark's phone, as I hadn't spoken with him for a few days. My message said, "ET phone home…" No reply. At 6:50 p.m., I typed the word "Call." In between texts, I also placed several calls to his number. The phone went straight to voicemail. This was somewhat unusual, as this generally means a phone has been turned off or has run out of battery, and Mark always kept his phone on and charged. Another unsuccessful phone call was followed by more texts, including one that said, "Call home, or I will drive up there," and later, "Why is your phone going straight to voicemail? Call home now." I never received a response. At 8:07 p.m., I texted again: "I have been calling and texting you since 4:45 p.m. with no response. You need to call home immediately. Where are you? Why is your phone off?"

It was unusual for Mark to ignore my calls and texts; however, I wasn't terribly concerned since I knew he'd been scheduled to work at the campus bar the previous evening. I thought he might be napping and had muted his phone. I called and texted a few more times before turning in early for bed. I woke at 11:00 p.m. and checked my phone. No response. I don't think I slept again. I just lay there, entertaining the idea of making the brief drive to campus.

At 12:13 a.m., Thursday, March 8, I texted the following message: "Call my phone or Guy's. We are up." I continued to lay awake, going over scenarios in my mind. I texted again a little while later: "It is almost 1:00 a.m., and I am thinking about driving up there. Please call home now."

After that text, I got out of bed and headed to the great room. I turned on the computer, as I considered calling the Miami University Police Department and wanted his address. I knew the dorm and location of his room but wanted to jot down the exact information in case I needed it. After locating the address on his student account, I continued to peruse the page. I scrolled down a bit and got to his dining hall account. He hadn't swiped out for meals since Monday, March 5, nearly three days earlier. I knew then something serious was amiss, as the boy ate every day.

In an effort to scare him into replying, I sent my final text to him at approximately 1:35 a.m.: "I am calling the

Miami police if I don't hear from you within fifteen minutes. That will be at 1:52 a.m."

I didn't wait the fifteen minutes, as my mind raced with worry and gloomy thoughts. A knot developed in my abdomen, and a wave of panic washed over me. I called the Miami University Police Department and spoke with a female officer. I told her I'd been attempting to contact my son since late afternoon with no response. I let her know it wasn't typical for Mark to blow off my texts and calls and that he lived with type 1 diabetes. She typed his name into her computer and learned he hadn't swiped out of his room since Monday. She told me she was dispatching an officer to his room immediately. I told her my husband and I lived close and we would jump in the car and head that way. I turned off the computer and woke up my husband, filling him in. As we both threw on clothes, I remember repeating the words, "Something terrible has happened. Something terrible has happened." As I sat at the computer just minutes before, learning my son hadn't eaten or left his room for over two days, I was certain he'd either passed away or had gone missing.

As Guy and I began the trek to campus, I quietly and fearfully pondered the possible reasons for Mark's silence. About fifteen minutes into the drive, I realized I hadn't received a return phone call from the campus police. I dialed their number and was connected with a male officer. I asked him for an update. He sidestepped my question and suggested we come directly to the police station. I had a feeling he knew something about Mark, so I asked him again if he had any information and let him know I wasn't driving. His reply changed the course of my life forever: "Ma'am, I am sorry to inform you that your son is deceased."

My worst nightmare unfolded on that frigid March morning as I rode shotgun through the dark and desolate streets. My body began to shake, not from the freezing temperatures but from shock. As the sun rose on that late winter day, I continued to shake and shiver as my mind attempted to chip away at and decipher the events of that morning. My son and only child had left this world. He was twenty years, one month, and one day old.

chapter 9
Why?

Instead of wondering WHY this is happening to you, consider why this is happening to YOU.

—Dalai Lama

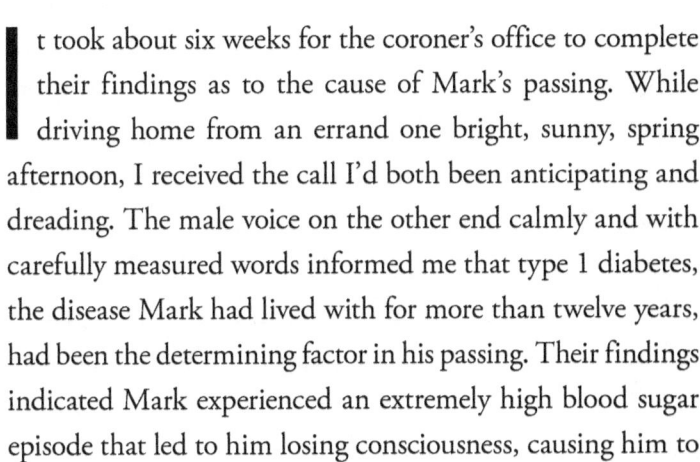

It took about six weeks for the coroner's office to complete their findings as to the cause of Mark's passing. While driving home from an errand one bright, sunny, spring afternoon, I received the call I'd both been anticipating and dreading. The male voice on the other end calmly and with carefully measured words informed me that type 1 diabetes, the disease Mark had lived with for more than twelve years, had been the determining factor in his passing. Their findings indicated Mark experienced an extremely high blood sugar episode that led to him losing consciousness, causing him to lapse into a diabetic coma where his body shut down. This is believed to be a rather peaceful and painless way to exit this world. For lack of better words, Mark went to sleep, never to awaken again. A Miami University police officer who was present at the time Mark was found told us they located him just inside his dorm room, slumped over on the floor.

In the hours and days after his passing, we began to piece together a timeline of events and Mark sightings that had taken place between my last phone conversation with him on Saturday, March 3, and the later morning of Tuesday, March 6. It became apparent that a perfect storm of events had occurred that led up to Mark being alone and ill in his room.

When I phoned the campus police early Thursday morning, I was informed that Mark hadn't left his dorm room since sometime on Monday. When I initially heard this, I immediately thought not only of Mark, but I was also concerned about his roommate. When I asked the officer if Mark's roommate had been swiping in and out of the room, she informed me he wasn't enrolled at the university. I was completely stunned and at a loss for words upon hearing this, as Mark neglected to share this information with us. We soon learned the roommate had moved out on Saturday, March 3, and Mark had helped him remove his things from their shared space. I believe Mark intentionally kept this information from us, as we wouldn't have been in favor of him living alone, even for a brief amount of time, without putting certain safety measures into place.

A college campus is a big place with hundreds of dorm rooms. It's impossible to expect some sort of policing of the comings and goings of thousands of students who may or may not be swiping in and out of their room. Also, many instructors don't take attendance and, therefore, are unaware of students who miss class. The fact that Mark had passed away alone in his dorm room didn't cause a blip on the radar of any university personnel, at least not in those first thirty-six hours.

We also learned Mark hadn't been feeling well on Monday, but instead of phoning me or Guy for advice or help, he reached out to friends. Sometime in the late afternoon, Mark contacted a friend for suggestions on how to remedy a major headache. This person instructed him to take a shower, lie down, and avoid spending time on any screens. Another friend did go to dinner with Mark Monday night and then accompanied him back to his room. The friend suggested Mark check his blood sugar; however, when he couldn't readily locate his meter, he blew off this necessary bedtime ritual, choosing instead to settle in for the night oblivious to his number. The severe headache Mark experienced was most likely directly related to his diabetes, as this can be a sign of either a high or low blood sugar. Mark knew he needed to rule out diabetes as the cause of his headache, and this could've been easily and quickly done with the prick of his finger. After Mark's passing, I had a chance to go through his meter, where I determined he'd been experiencing extremely high blood sugars. This was most likely the result of eating and not injecting the appropriate amount of insulin, not taking any insulin at all, or neglecting to take his once-a-day, long-acting insulin, Lantus.

The world of diabetes care and management has experienced significant and life-changing strides in recent years due in large part to technological advances. One such advancement is the Continuous Glucose Monitoring system, CGM for short. The CGM is a device that tracks blood glucose levels through interstitial fluid day and night and shares the data with a transmitter or smartphone. The CGM user inserts a tiny sensor wire just under their skin by using an applicator, and an adhesive patch holds the sensor in place. In May 2017, after returning home at the end of his freshman year, Mark agreed to wear a CGM as a way to have more awareness of his blood sugar readings as well as eliminating his twelve-year reliance on finger sticks and a meter. The CGM model Mark used required a calibration of the device every twelve hours, and these became the only two required blood sugar readings Mark needed to complete by using his lancet device and meter. For an individual living with type 1 diabetes, finger sticks can range from a recommended minimum of four per day up to eight or more if necessary.

It didn't take Mark long to become acquainted with his CGM, and he seemed pleased with the information it was able to share. He was provided blood sugar readings every five minutes on his smartphone, and thanks to a sharing app, his numbers were sent to my phone as well. The device has an alarm that beeps when a blood sugar reading goes outside the range set up by the wearer. Mark's range was set at 70 to 140. If his blood sugar began trending below a reading of 70—a number considered on the safe side of the lower range—both of our phones would beep. This same scenario occurred if his blood sugar rose above a reading of 140. The alarm serves as a signal that certain measures might need to be taken to prevent a low or high blood sugar from occurring. If the 24/7 information provided by the CGM is used properly as a means of maintaining blood sugars in a normal range, it can greatly assist in achieving A1C levels that are at or below acceptable levels.

The A1C is a blood test that reflects one's average blood glucose levels over a three-month period. The target A1C for someone Mark's age is 7.0 or less. For the first several years Mark lived with diabetes, his A1C tests indicated results that were within acceptable levels for his age. This changed in high school, as Mark began to slack off with his diabetes care. Numbers that once ranged from 7.5 to 8.0 crept up to 9, 10, and higher. Having prolonged A1C numbers at the higher levels can contribute to long-term complications, such as eye damage (retinopathy), kidney damage (nephropathy), nerve damage (neuropathy), and foot and skin issues. During a routine visit to the diabetes clinic in November 2017, Mark learned his A1C was 6.9. This was the lowest reading he'd ever achieved in all of the years he lived with this dreadful disease. To say Mark was ecstatic upon learning this number would be putting it mildly. He phoned me immediately upon leaving the clinic appointment to share the great news. I later learned he'd shared this information with several friends as well. It seemed he was back on track with his diabetes care and was excited about maintaining his health. We could've never known this would be his last A1C test.

Sometime during the day on Friday, March 2, 2018, Mark's CGM quit sending readings to my phone. I texted him about this issue and also questioned him about it on Saturday morning when we spoke. I instructed him to figure out what the problem was and get it fixed. When he continued to neglect this issue, I emailed him Sunday morning and brought it up again. For some reason, Mark seemed unconcerned and unwilling to remedy the problem. In hindsight, I could've demanded he either replace the CGM sensor or figure out the problem, or else he'd have to return home until he could get it working again. I failed to do this. I'll never know the reason why Mark suddenly became negligent with his diabetes care after achieving his best-ever A1C result just months earlier. I can only assume he rationalized some sort of false sense of security that his diabetes was in check and, therefore, he could afford to slack off. If he'd thought about it, he would've recalled that the A1C is a highly variable number. It can quickly go up or down, depending on one's day-to-day care.

I'll likely never know the actual reason why Mark failed to reach out to us when he began feeling ill, though I have my suspicions. About two weeks before Mark's passing, we drove to campus and took him out to lunch. Mark had only been back at school for a few weeks following the lengthy winter break. It was during this visit that I shared my perceptions of Mark's college experience thus far. I specifically said the words, "You're in over your head up here." I then went on to spell out three possible scenarios I was considering regarding his immediate future and the pursuit of a college degree. The first one involved Mark returning home, where he would finish out the semester as a commuting student. The second scenario included a complete withdrawal from the university for at least this one semester. During this time off, Mark would work at least part-time and prove he was taking care of his diabetes as well as discontinuing any use of alcohol or marijuana. The third option involved him withdrawing from Miami and reapplying to his second-choice school, the University of Cincinnati. I was calm and collected as I shared these options with him, and I think he was beginning to believe we were no longer going to allow him to remain caught up in his gerbil-wheel existence. It was time for him to hop off and put an end to his apparent refusal to learn from his mistakes.

Later, as I reflected back on that lunchtime conversation, I think Mark did take my words to heart and was scared I'd follow through with one of my scenarios if he continued to display signs he wasn't getting his act together. If we'd been made aware he wasn't feeling well, Mark correctly assumed we would make the short drive to campus. If we'd shown up at his dorm room, we would've realized he was living alone, a situation that wasn't in Mark's best interest, given his sketchy diabetes care as well as other behaviors. An unexpected visit such as this most likely would've resulted in a temporary end to Mark's college career or in him forfeiting his opportunity to live on campus.

Mark made it through the night on what would become his last Monday on Earth and apparently continued to feel bad. In the late morning of Tuesday, March 6, Mark sent what was likely his final text message. I don't know the exact words contained within this text, only that it was somewhat incoherent. The friend on the receiving end was otherwise occupied and innocently shrugged off the message as a groggy text from his friend who was just waking up.

It is my firm belief Mark sent that text as he began to lose consciousness and very soon after he drifted into a coma. As he slumped to the floor, his body began to shut down, allowing him to slip quietly from this lifetime. It seems possible Mark had no idea he was making a fatal mistake by not reaching out to me or by not calling 911. In all the years Mark and I had lived with diabetes, he'd never experienced an extremely low or high blood sugar level that resulted in taking extreme measures to prevent a coma or even death. Mark didn't have decent numbers for a lengthy period of time; however, nothing had ever gotten so bad that I or someone else had to call for help, nor had we ever had to use the Glucagon pen we always kept on hand in case of an extreme low. Glucagon is a prescription medication used to treat a life-threatening low blood sugar, otherwise known as severe hypoglycemia. It's injected into a diabetic who has either passed out or cannot ingest some form of sugar by mouth. We purchased but never used at least twenty-five Glucagon pens over the years. When the medication reached its expiration date, it was tossed and replaced by new pens kept both at home and at school. It would never be a good idea to wish a coma or close call on any diabetic; however, looking back, I feel that since Mark hadn't ever been confronted with the extreme danger of life with diabetes, he was completely unaware and unprepared for the urgency a severe low or high blood sugar can create. And more so, he was naive to how quickly things can deteriorate, often resulting in no chance for survival. Alone in his room, he was incapable of taking care of himself and the dire situation. In other words, he had no chance to live to tell about it, much less learn from it.

After Mark passed, he remained on his dorm room floor until I reached out to the university police. He was incommunicado for well over thirty-six hours, and I still wonder why none of his friends thought this was odd or out of character for him. As far as I know, Mark interacted with his friends and classmates daily, either via text or in person, and even shared classes with a few of them. I also believe he never dined alone and, therefore, would've reached out to people at mealtimes. I know at least one friend texted Mark during this time, receiving no response. Apparently, Mark's status as MIA didn't trigger a cause for concern within his small circle of friends. And this lack of communication is true for me as well. I knew Mark had been scheduled to work on Tuesday night at his new job, so when I didn't hear from him Tuesday or during the day on Wednesday, I chalked it up to him being busy and tired. Also, since Mark's roommate had contacted us in the past when he was concerned about Mark and his diabetes, I had no reason to believe this backup safety measure was no longer in place. It never entered my mind that Mark was living alone.

I don't share this deeply personal and troubling chain of events as a way of placing blame on anyone for their inaction or inability to assess the seriousness of Mark's health predicament, including the university, as this is an exercise in futility. I want to make it perfectly clear I don't hold anyone accountable for Mark's passing. Period. Mark had all of the medication and supplies necessary to take care of his condition, including the means to test for and remedy a high blood sugar. He also knew we were available to him 24/7. We'd made three trips to campus for minor things just the week before. For some unknown reason, he chose not to save himself. Why? I've literally begged for an answer to this question countless times in the days, weeks, and months since Mark left us. As I traverse my journey of grief, I know I must surrender to the fact this question will most likely remain unanswered, and I must also forgive myself for not removing him from a situation that was far too much for him to handle.

Sometime toward the end of Mark's freshman year, he shared with us that he didn't come home often because it stirred up feelings of homesickness, which then made it difficult to return to school. We took this as a kind of backhanded compliment, one that revealed he actually enjoyed being around us. I've reflected on Mark's comment often in the time since his passing and wish I'd read more into it back then. It seems possible Mark would've had more of an opportunity to grow and mature had he attended college as a commuter, at least for the first two years or so, and I could've continued to monitor his diabetes care. This was even suggested to Mark by his long-time nurse practitioner during a clinic visit in his senior year in high school. But as always, hindsight can be 20/20, and I must toss all of my "woulda, coulda, shouldas" into the wind, setting them and myself free of the burden and waste of time that is regret.

So just like that, our Trifecta of Trauma morphed into a Quadruple Quagmire. In the span of twenty years and a smattering of days, the Hyams trio was dismantled, leaving me to make some sort of sense of what still feels like a horrific nightmare. In what direction does one go when faced with things in life that can't be easily explained or understood?

The answer, I believe, lies partly in faith. My current beliefs weren't derived from a traditional source, such as organized religion, but instead were birthed from an understanding that there's someone or something greater than us, an architect and overseer of our life plan. And this being doesn't work alone. This essence or entity is aided in this divine work by the help of angels, guides, and a few feathered friends.

Part 3

The Divine Within and Around Us

Trust in Divine timing…it's a spiritual synchronicity.
The alignment of people, places and events
choreographed for your soul's highest good.

—Muses from a Mystic

chapter 10
A Segue into Secularism

I believe in God, but not as one thing, not as an old man in the sky. I believe that what people call God is something in all of us.

—John Lennon

I was raised in a laid-back Catholic home. I had both a baptism and confirmation, and I attended CCD classes, an acronym for Confraternity of Christian Doctrine or "church school," at our local parish. We were mostly "holiday Catholics," faithfully showing up for Christmas and Easter with the obligatory Sunday or Saturday matinee attendance tossed in here and there. I also recall participating in the occasional ritual of confession, where a parishioner has the opportunity for a one-on-one purge with a priest.

When it came time for me to rid myself of my earthly transgressions, I often hiked the short distance to the church from our home, patiently waited my turn, and then entered what was basically a dark, cramped closet. I sat on the hard, cool seat, nervously anticipating the sliding of a little door, revealing a screen separating the father from the sinner. The priest would ask the purpose of my visit, and I'd begin to recite my wrongdoings, most of which concerned the use of certain curse words as well as talking behind my mother's back while sometimes making hand or finger gestures. I completed my sin-filled purge and then found my way to the pews to complete my penance. I knelt on the padded bench, closed my eyes, and recited the "Our Father" and "Hail Mary" from memory. I never cheated on the number of recitations that were part of my penance thanks in large part to fear, and in the eyes of a child, this fear is not unwarranted. Fibbing in the house of God while one atones for sins could very well result in lightning bolts striking the wooden structure, igniting a huge fire, which would result in an immediate and painful passing for all of the wretched souls trapped inside. We wouldn't burn in hell but would already be crispy fried as we crossed over. I had no intention of rocketing from this lifetime engulfed in flames. I dutifully completed my prayers, stood, and exited via the side door, believing I'd reserved my spot in heaven. At least, that is, until I started cussing again.

As an adult, I reflected back on all of the hours spent in religion class, services, and confession and realized I'd failed to absorb the teachings the Catholic Church offered in regard to Christianity, the Bible, and a supposed judgmental God whom we're supposed to fear. Perhaps this was due to the fact that a Catholic mass is a bit of a workout, what with all the sit, stand, kneel, form a line for communion, etc. Most likely, I was so busy paying attention to all of the holy calisthenics that I couldn't mentally absorb the religious teachings of the day. Also, during the homily portion of the service—one of the lengthier periods of rest—I'm certain my mind drifted to nonholy topics, such as what I was doing after church or what congregants were up to in the pews in front of me. Instead of daydreaming and worrying about little Johnny fidgeting in front of me, I should've been all ears while the priest droned on about the day's gospel and its divine message. Looking back, I'm certain my main objective on any given Sunday was to make it through the one-hour mass, dip my fingers into the holy water located near the exit, and head for the car, all while making the ritualistic sign of the cross.

While my parents did their best to raise me as a decent, obedient Catholic, school history classes and my own bookworm habits introduced me to World War II, the Holocaust, Judaism, Anne Frank, and more. My parents, both born and raised in Germany, were in their late teens when war broke out in the mother country. My father enlisted in the German army upon turning eighteen. He never discussed much about the war; however, he did engage in battle on the Russian front. The scars on his shoulders, engraved by grazing bullets, were physical proof of his service. My mother's family lived in Berlin during the war and lost nearly everything during the conflict. She and my grandmother often sold treasured family heirlooms to buy food and other basic necessities. Decades after the end of this horrific and dark period in history, my mother could still vividly recall the sound of the sirens, warning residents of incoming enemy bomb attacks.

Even though I was aware of some of the tough times my parents lived through during the war, I still occasionally felt embarrassed about being born into a German family. My parents weren't Nazis, but so many people equate all Germans with the horrors carried out by Hitler and his evil cronies. Through reading, I identified with Jews and their plight. It wasn't until college that I acted on the connection I felt for Jewish people and their repeated history of persecution. As a young student at North Texas State University, now known as the University of North Texas, I secretly joined the Jewish Student's Association. I say secretly, as no one asked if I was Jewish, so I never informed them I wasn't. This was the Hebrew version of "Don't Ask, Don't Tell." As a member of this organization, I attended meetings, passed out flyers about upcoming events, and served as the secretary/public relations person. It was during this time I began to consider converting to Judaism. I became connected with a Dallas-area rabbi and was fortunate to have a few one-on-one meetings with him. He spoke kindly and candidly with me about his religion, answered questions, and provided me with reading material to peruse at home. I never converted, as once again, an organized religion wasn't filling my spiritual cup. I did, however, find a way to incorporate Judaism into my life. This *shiksah* met and married a true *mensch* a few years later.

My spiritual quest continued from my late twenties into my early thirties. I always maintained a belief in God or a higher power; however, I couldn't find my footing within the confines of organized religion. Sometime in the late '80s, I made one last ditch effort to reconnect with my Catholic roots. I attended a Sunday mass at a local church, its pews filled with couples and families. As I sat alone on the hard, wooden pew, completing the ritual holy calisthenics, something didn't feel right. I could follow along with the service, but I wasn't getting anything from it. I was unable to personally connect with what was being preached and how it pertained to my life. At the end of the service, my spiritual tank remained on empty, leaving me without a holy home.

My status as a wandering Catholic and unconverted Jew remained intact even after my marriage to Alan. He never asked me to convert, though it was his wish Mark be raised Jewish. Mark had a *bris*—also known as a *brit milah*—the Jewish ceremony of circumcision, usually performed on an infant's eighth day of life. Due to Mark's premature birth, this ritual was delayed until he was about a month old. Mark was given a Hebrew name, Velvel, and Alan hoped this was the first of many Jewish rites of passage for his son. Not long before Alan passed, we had a conversation about religion. I let him know I didn't feel comfortable raising Mark in the Jewish faith, nor was it my intention to raise him as Catholic either. I intended to let Mark decide if he wanted to follow a religious path, one that might include Judaism. This decision would be his and his alone. Perhaps he'd set out on his own spiritual quest, and, like mine, this quest might last well into adulthood. My own search for soul went on rather aimlessly until God placed two women in my path who'd become my spiritual mentors.

I met Sandra and Susan almost simultaneously, and my life has never been the same. Sandra was the person responsible for giving me my first job when I made a career switch from retail to corporate fitness. I met Susan not long after beginning my new position when I attended a class she was teaching that fulfilled CEU requirements for my aerobics instructor and personal trainer certifications. These two old souls and kindred spirits were the spark that ignited my spiritual epiphany, one no organized religion had been able to awaken or arouse. Over the past two decades, I've devoured hordes of spiritual books and magazine articles and have met dozens of like-minded individuals who've wandered into my path.

It appears I wasn't alone in my questioning of organized religion and the Catholic faith that had been bestowed upon me with my baptism. There's been a significant and constant decline in attendance of religious services across all faiths for some time now. Google "decline in religion," and several articles and published studies pop up to explain this global, dramatic, and downward shift in participation in organized religion. There appear to be many factors contributing to this phenomenon; however, much of it can be explained by the fact that people are becoming more secular. *Merriam-Webster* defines *secular* as "not overtly or specifically religious." In a post on his blog on October 20, 2017, Allen Downey, a professor at Olin College, said this: "According to the Theory of Secularization, as societies become more modern, they become less religious. Aspects of secularization include decreasing participation in organized religion, loss of religious belief, and declining respect for religious authority."

The appearance of Sandra and Susan in my life came a few years prior to Alan's diagnosis. Alone and adrift with no real spiritual mooring, I finally found my way to teachings and philosophies that resulted in my aha moment. I identified with a handful of beliefs that made sense to me. These broad yet simple principles provided me with a template about how to live my life as well as a greater understanding of the purpose of my human journey.

chapter 11
Religion of Joan

We are not human beings having a spiritual experience.
We are spiritual beings having a human experience.

—Pierre Teilhard de Chardin

Spiritual, not religious. These are the words I use to describe myself in regard to the divine. Again, I want to reinforce I'm not sharing my faith as a way to dismiss or question anyone's belief system. I'm merely sharing the tools that have aided me in making some sort of sense of my life and all that's transpired. You don't have to agree with my philosophies; however, if nothing else, perhaps they can serve as food for thought.

Using the vast amount of information I gathered from my readings and encounters with others, I formulated a set of ideas I lovingly and tongue-in-cheek refer to as "the religion of joan." (Lowercase letters are intentional.) There are few doctrines or tenets in my church. Instead, I maintain a simple list of beliefs that serve as an instruction manual for me on how to navigate life and its many lessons. There are nine tenets in the religion of joan:

1. I believe in a Higher Power
2. *Everything* Happens for a Reason
3. We All Are One
4. We Are Made of Energy
5. Humans Are a Trinity—Body, Mind, and Spirit
6. There Are Only Two Emotions—Love and Fear
7. We Are Here as Both Student and Teacher
8. When Your Time on Earth Is Up, It Is Up
9. Nothing Dies

The tenets are self-explanatory; however, I'll provide a brief synopsis of each one.

1. **I Believe in a Higher Power.** You can refer to he or she however you choose: God, the Holy One, Love, etc. I most often use the term *God* because a vast majority of people instantly recognize whom this term refers to. I believe he or she is love in its purest form and possesses the highest degree of light and vibration. I occasionally pray to this God and believe he or she is listening, watching,

and even guiding but doesn't judge. When we're in human form, it's our soul's purpose to experience growth that elevates us to a higher light and vibration level each time we visit Earth. I believe we are granted some amount of free will in how we choose to live our lives. However, there are many aspects of human life that aren't within our control. This is where tenet number two comes into play.

2. **Everything Happens for a Reason.** I don't believe in fate, luck, chance, or accidents. The universe is perfect! Every single situation and encounter we find ourselves in is meant to be even when it defies our human understanding, logic, and ego. Deepak Chopra says, "Trust that your soul has a plan, and even if you can't see it completely, know that everything will unfold as it is meant to."

    Life is full of peaks and valleys. The valleys of life are our opportunities to achieve personal growth. If we're able to embrace our challenges and dive headfirst into them, we are fulfilling our soul's purpose. While we may never come to know the true reason or reasons why certain events occur, we may find comfort and strength in trusting this was meant to be. We must then squeeze all we can out of the lesson and simply let it go. One of my favorite mantras is, "Let go, let God."

3. **We All Are One.** We are all connected, and we're here to love and help one another. Period. We came

from the same place, and when we leave here, we will return to the same place. It seems while we're in human form, we often lose sight of our interconnectedness, and this might be the result of labels we place on ourselves and others. It's my opinion that once we begin labeling ourselves and others as male or female, black or white, gay or straight, rich or poor, white collar or blue collar, Republican or Democrat, conservative or liberal, Christian or Jewish, or Buddhist or Muslim, we head down the dangerous path of distancing ourselves from one another. Each label creates a barrier. The more labels, the more barriers. We also reinforce our disconnect by the borders we delineate and the walls we build. This isn't a political statement. It's a spiritual observation. There's only one race—the human race—and we've repeatedly failed to respect one another and get along, which is why we live in the absence of peace.

One of my favorite spiritual beings is the musician, lyricist, and hippie John Lennon who cowrote the iconic song "Imagine." The words penned decades ago still have meaning and purpose today. And we, the humans who currently inhabit this planet, have yet to fulfill John's dream. The last line of the song is "And the world will be as one." And so I believe it's the late John Lennon who best sums up tenet number three: we all are one.

4. **We Are All Made of Energy.** I believe with my very nonscientific mind this energy is actually light energy. Another term for this is "aura." In 2007, I happened to be watching an episode of *The Oprah Winfrey Show*. Her guest was John Diaz, one of ninety-six survivors of a Singapore Airlines plane crash that occurred in October 2000. As John and the others made their way out of the aircraft, he turned and looked toward the back of the plane where a few passengers were literally being burned alive in the flames ignited by jet fuel that had sprayed the cabin. He noticed some people had a dim light or aura around them, while others had a much larger, brighter light surrounding them. At that moment, he decided he wanted "To live my life so that when I leave, my aura will be bright."

I've never forgotten that show, as I know I was meant to see it and hear John's story. I believe our aura is related to where we are in our spiritual growth process and often delineates baby souls from old souls. It seems appropriate to share a little about my belief in reincarnation, though I generally don't use that term. I believe our spirit makes hundreds of trips to Earth, toting luggage containing specific and concrete plans aimed at achieving spiritual growth, thus elevating one's light (aura) and vibration (energy). It's possible younger souls, ones who've had fewer incarnations and/or have experienced fewer lessons, possess a dimmer aura. Older souls, the ones who've made numerous trips to Earth and/or have experienced tremendous growth, often possess a brighter aura and a higher vibration. Nikola Tesla sums it up this way: "If you want to find the secrets of the universe, think in terms of energy, frequency and vibration."

I agree with John Diaz in that how we choose to live our life while on this planet contributes to the brightness and thickness of our light. I believe if we live a life of kindness and empathy and make the best attempt to embrace all of our challenges and opportunities for growth while in human form, we can greatly enhance the luminosity of our aura.

As a side note, I recently obtained a reading of my aura and found it to be spot on. Without going into a lot of boring detail, my aura reader shared this: "I know what I believe in spiritually," which offered me confirmation that I'm a devoted and devout follower of the religion of my creation. She also shared that our aura can fluctuate, depending on our life circumstances. I took that to mean if we continually evolve and grow while in human form, we have the ability to alter our aura in a positive manner.

5. **Humans Are a Trinity—Body, Mind, and Spirit.** We must nurture all three for optimum health. This includes taking care of ourselves with proper diet and exercise, seeking out professional help if necessary for mental challenges, and making time for faith,

including attending services as well as engaging in meditation, reading, volunteering, and connecting with others. We can rid our bodies of negative emotions by crying, yelling, talking, hitting a pillow, journaling, and more. If we focus on just one aspect of our being, we risk exposing ourselves to an imbalance, making it possible for illness to slither in. Shakti Gawain said, "Our bodies communicate to us clearly and specifically *if* we are willing to listen."

Sometime in the mid-1990s, my spiritual mentor Sandra gifted me with a copy of *The Bodymind Workbook* by Debbie Shapiro. This gem was first published in Great Britain decades ago; however, the information and insights contained within remain current and valuable. If there were one text that could serve as the bible for the religion of joan, this would be it. The book explores how the mind and body work together and explains the connection between the two both in times of good health as well as in times of illness. I've referred to Ms. Shapiro's words countless times over the years, and I found her information to be spot on when I was diagnosed with leukemia. I firmly believe my buried grief and anger surrounding Alan's cancer diagnosis and passing contributed to my illness. As a means of ridding my body of this blood cancer, I took the Western medicine and also met with a therapist, journaled, exercised, cleaned up my diet, devoured books, and meditated. It was critically important to me that I survived, as I didn't want my son to become an orphan. I believe my tremendous will coupled with my holistic treatments greatly contributed to my healing and cure as I regained balance of my trinity.

6. **There Are Only Two Emotions—Love and Fear.** Our purpose on Earth is to love and be loved. Period. When we're acting or reacting in a place devoid of love, we are living in fear, which is disguised as anger, bitterness, jealousy, guilt, insecurity, hate, judgment, arrogance, and victim consciousness to name a few. We must constantly and consistently ask ourselves if we're operating out of a place of love or fear. This simple question permits us to stop and consider our thoughts and actions and can aid us in making the right choices that will enable our growth and provide for a more joyful and fulfilling life.

7. **We Are Here as Both Student and Teacher.** If you combine this concept with tenet number two, it might explain a lot. If we arrive here with some sort of divine agenda, then everything that happens to us is meant to either teach us something or provide us with an opportunity to influence the path of another. In the words of Paulo Coelho, "Important encounters are planned by the souls long before the bodies see each other."

It's through our countless, nonrandom encounters with others that we're presented with opportunities for growth as well as the ability to increase our light and vibration.

8. **When Your Time on Earth Is Up, It Is Up.** I believe when a soul plans its return to human form, the birthdate or arrival date isn't random. Neither is an end date. When all of our intended lessons and teachings are complete, the bell rings, signifying the end of class, and the soul returns home. Notice I didn't use the word "died." This leads to the ninth and final tenet.

9. **Nothing Dies.** I often use the phrase "No one is getting out of here alive," when discussing or bringing awareness to the human concept of death. However, since we're all made of energy, we never actually "die." We merely change form. We trade one life or existence for another. To put it simply, we move.

Many years ago, I read the book *The Seat of the Soul* by Gary Zukav. Within these pages, I was introduced to the concept of the "earth suit." My physical presence as Joan, white female of German descent, is the costume I chose to wear in this lifetime as I complete my karmic lessons and teachings. When my work on Earth is complete, I'll shed my "earth suit" or shell and return to my pure, positive, energetic form. Throughout my daily life, I make a conscious effort to dismiss the terms "die" and "died" from my vocabulary, as *nothing* dies. The term "death" invokes feelings of negativity and implies that we're finite. We are infinite, divine beings created in the image of love and light.

I've been a faithful, devoted leader and follower of the religion of joan. I lovingly refer to myself as the sole parishioner in a belief system I came to subscribe to over the course of many years. After grappling with the concepts taught by organized religion, I found a way back to what my soul has known all along. I'm not a human having a spiritual experience. I'm a spiritual being having a human experience. Deepak Chopra describes the difference between the two in this way: "Religion is the belief in someone else's experience. Spirituality is having your own experience."

These tenets or guidelines have proven to be my life jacket of sorts. They served as the buoy I clung to as life took a few dramatic and tragic turns. The Hyams family—Alan, Joan, and Mark—were three humans living out a plan divinely crafted long ago. Together, we charted a course filled with adversity that became an extreme test of our strength and resilience as well as a front row seat in the school of life. And since we were living out this karmic arrangement in an earthly state of amnesia, we had no idea what was heading our way. Two members of this unit have shed their earth suits and returned to spirit form. Their time here was up, as their mission was complete. However, they didn't travel far. Alan and Mark are still around. And I have proof.

chapter 12
Signs and Symbols

Life is one big road with lots of signs.

—Bob Marley

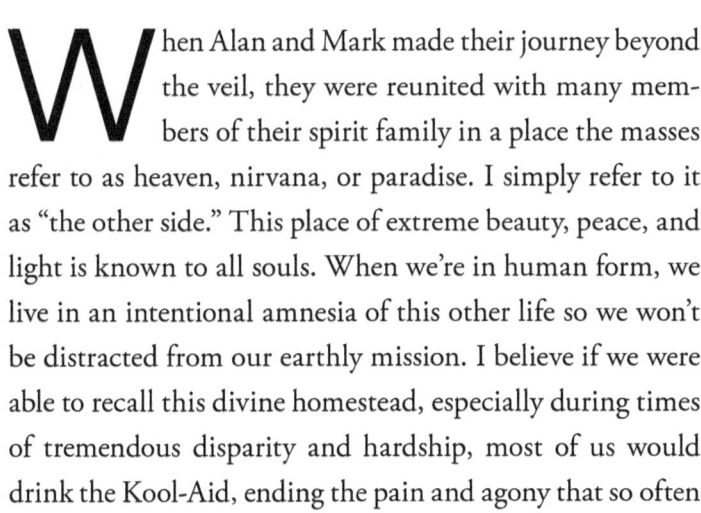

When Alan and Mark made their journey beyond the veil, they were reunited with many members of their spirit family in a place the masses refer to as heaven, nirvana, or paradise. I simply refer to it as "the other side." This place of extreme beauty, peace, and light is known to all souls. When we're in human form, we live in an intentional amnesia of this other life so we won't be distracted from our earthly mission. I believe if we were able to recall this divine homestead, especially during times of tremendous disparity and hardship, most of us would drink the Kool-Aid, ending the pain and agony that so often challenges us when we're in physical form. We'd exit this hell on earth and follow the light to this place far beyond human comprehension. There are some living among us who are blessed with opportunities to capture a glimpse of this special place. These precious peeks into this other life can come during meditation, near-death experiences, or some other enlightened or heightened state of consciousness.

As I mentioned, we're all made of energy. In fact, everything in the universe is made of energy, and this energy vibrates at different frequencies. Humans vibrate at a slower frequency than those residing beyond the veil. Individuals who are practiced in meditation often gain the ability to raise their vibration, elevating it to a level or frequency that permits them to connect with the other side. With that said, one doesn't have to master meditation in an effort to connect with our spiritual self or others. Spending quiet time alone, which might include a walk in nature, enables us to send and receive messages and gain insight into our journey. In a blog post, Nikki Sharp said this: "Listen and silent are spelled with the same letters."

There also exist individuals, such as psychics and mediums, who arrive here with otherworldly abilities. We all possess some level of psychic ability, often referred to as our sixth sense; however, some of us are more gifted in their capabilities than others. If the term "psychic" sounds too new age or cheesy or evokes a negative connotation of some sort, then perhaps the terms "intuition" (as in mother's intuition), "gut feeling," and "ESP" (extrasensory perception) can be used to explain our ability to gain information via our mind rather than our five physical senses.

I've known for some time that we are able to engage in communication with souls who've made the transition to the other side. There are many ways in which messages can be sent and received if you allow yourself to believe. One of the most common methods spirits utilize to let us know they're around is the concept of "pennies from heaven." As we go about our daily life, it's not uncommon to happen upon a random coin—a penny, nickel, dime, or quarter—that has ended up in our path. According to the psychic medium Blair Robertson, our spirit family wants us to know we are loved and valued, and one of the ways they convey this message is via a one-cent coin. He explains that pennies have the numerology or angel value of one and shares, "The angel number one is a reminder that we are all one. We are one with spirit. Love never dies."

In the time since Mark's passing, I've happened upon a penny here and there, and so have other family members and friends who also believe in these tokens of love. If you stumble upon such a coin, consider it a sign from the other side. I encourage you to pick it up and ask yourself, "Who might have sent this to me?" The first person who enters your mind is most likely the sender. You should then acknowledge this found treasure with a thank-you. Also, you might want to find some sort of container in which to store these precious and priceless gifts from heaven, as many more might end up in your path.

Mark has also chosen electricity as a way to let us know he hangs around our home. Just days after his passing, Mark used his Honda Accord as a vehicle to connect with us. One evening as we prepared to sit down for dinner, the alarm in his car went off. I grabbed my car keys, opened the front door, and clicked the alarm button, resulting in immediate silence. The ensuing quiet turned out to be short lived, as a few minutes later, the alarm was tripped again. I jumped up from my seat, grabbed my keys, and pressed the button that brought an end to this familiar, piercing, and annoying sound.

This same scenario repeated itself several times in the coming days, with the final stint occurring one Saturday at the ungodly hour of 1:00 a.m. I was awakened from sleep by this familiar prank and knew Mark was announcing his presence yet again. I roused my sound-sleeping husband, alerting him to the honking. He jumped out of bed, threw on some pants, and headed outside to end the racket that disrupted the peaceful slumber of the neighborhood. Using the key fob, he disengaged the alarm and decided it was time for a more permanent method of ending these spirit games, at least for the night. He unhooked the car's battery, making it impossible for the alarm to be triggered, thus restoring a sleepy silence to the cul-de-sac. In the morning, we removed the few possessions that remained in the car—the garage door remote, an umbrella, and insurance paperwork—and then left the car unlocked in its spot on the driveway. This put the kibosh on this particular prank.

However, Mark would soon bring his games inside our home where he's used light fixtures (lamps and battery-operated signs), an iPod player, and a clock as ways to let us know he's around. Again, like pennies from heaven, one should always acknowledge these visits with a thank-you. This lets your loved ones know you appreciate and recognize their communication even if these encounters briefly disrupt the tranquility of your home. If a spirit believes their chosen form of communication incites fear or is unwelcome, they're less likely to continue such methods and might even discontinue their "visits."

As previously mentioned, I believe birds are spiritual creatures. They can serve as messengers of impending tragedy that might be visited upon an unsuspecting individual or family; however, they're most often used by our departed loved ones for more positive and uplifting interactions. We live in a suburban neighborhood complete with rows of houses, each with their own parcel of land. We're blessed to have a creek and brush line in our backyard, which provide easy access to nature as well as some semblance of privacy from the neighbors residing behind us. There are several pine trees rooted within this space. I recently spent time in the company of a Native American shaman and spiritual teacher, where I learned about the pine tree as a symbol of peace. These majestic pillars of green are held within high esteem in other cultures as well, where they serve as symbols of fertility, longevity, virtue, wisdom, and solitude. They're known to be strong and stubborn and can bend to avoid breaking. They represent eternal life.

The towering, aged, forever-green giants and their deciduous friends that dot the landscape of my personal nature sanctuary serve as a pit stop and home to a variety of birds, including cardinals, blue jays, robins, sparrows, hawks, and the occasional owl and woodpecker. During warm weather months, this mini forest comes alive each dawn with the language, melodies, and music of these winged creatures. They spend much of their day flitting and flying about, hunting for food, tending to their nests, and socializing as well as conducting business within their community.

Not long after Mark's passing, the calendar flipped from winter to spring, and nature sprang to life in this mini oasis. The trees slowly began to awaken from their long winter nap, and their once bare branches sprouted buds that would uncurl as leaves of green. For some reason, scores of birds flocked to this small corner of my world. I began to take special notice of two such creatures, one petite and vibrant and the other large and powerful.

According to L. J. Innes, the term "cardinal" comes from the Latin word *cardo,* meaning "hinge" or "axis." "Like a door's hinge, the cardinal is the hinge on the doorway between Earth and Spirit. They carry messages back and forth." The male cardinal, easily recognizable with its lipstick-red feathers, has long been considered the most notable spiritual messenger.

A male and female cardinal spent many months living and thriving in and around our backyard. I had numerous sightings and encounters with this monogamous couple as they went about their business; however, it was the male that hung around me most often. In the morning, upon opening the blind covering a bathroom window, I often found Mr. Cardinal perched on a spindly pine, all decked out in his vivid color and glory. If I happened to be outside working in the yard, he would flit about me and then come to rest on a branch in our large maple tree, or he kept me in his scope from atop our roof. I acknowledged him as a representative from loved ones who've crossed over, most likely sent by my parents, Alan, or Mark. It doesn't really matter who sent him. It only matters that I recognized Mr. Cardinal as a messenger of love from souls I can no longer converse with, hug, or touch.

The cardinal couple wasn't alone in this bird sanctuary that had seemingly sprung up overnight. As the season of spring continued to burst with life, offering signs of growth and new beginnings, another birth prepared to take place high atop a large, aging pine tree just within our fence line. A momma hawk had not so randomly chosen our small plot of land as the perfect spot to build a nest and tend to her egg. I'd lost my son as she prepared to bring new life into this world. I watched her daily as she used our deck railing, fence posts, and the surrounding rooftops as her observation towers. She sat fixed like a statue, quiet and stone faced, using her superior and keen eyesight to survey the area for her next meal. Like a Tibetan monk engaged in meditation, she could remain still for long periods of time, transfixed in a peaceful state that was both instinctual and practiced. Hawks are spirit animals living among us, and they serve as instructors of patience and awareness. If one frequently spots a hawk, the bird might be delivering a message to see things from a higher perspective, to focus or sharpen one's observation skills. In other words, hawks that circle about might be encouraging an individual to improve their vision, enabling them to see the big picture. They may also arrive to teach us to be fearless, as fear isn't an emotion in their repertoire.

A bird's spiritual essence isn't the only trait that differentiates them from other creatures. Birds are the only animals that sport feathers, and feathers are metaphors. Native Americans believe feathers are gifts from the sky, a symbol of the heavens. Their existence invokes meanings pertaining to flight, transcendence, and escape and, according to Chris Maynard, can be a "bridge between two worlds." The term "light as a feather" can be a bit of a misnomer, as lightness can be confused with delicacy. Feathers are made of the protein keratin, the same material found within a bird's beak and claws. Feathers are tough yet graceful and majestic. And there's significance in their color and the message they carry.

White feathers are the most common and are sent as a sign of support from the other side, a reminder to take better care of yourself. Below is a list of additional feather colors and their meanings as defined by Radhika Mehrotra:

- Blue: An acceptance of self and speaking truth; a strong connection with the spirit realm
- Brown: Grounding, endurance, home, friendship, respect

- Gray: Neutrality and strong protection; have faith at all times
- Purple: Universal consciousness; heightened spiritual growth and experiences
- Yellow: Related to gut instinct, mental alertness, joy, cheerfulness, intelligence, playfulness
- Black: Can be a warning sign and is strong protection; signifies mystical wisdom—you are undergoing a spiritual initiation, growth, or increased wisdom

The rarer red feather has many significant meanings, including courage, life force, passion, power, and vitality. They can also be a sign you're becoming stronger, which can include gaining strength following a health issue. Red feathers might confirm you're heading in the right direction as you pursue some goal or complete a project. While working on this book, I happened upon three red feathers. I picked them up, acknowledged the sender with a thank-you, and brought them inside, where they're part of my meditation space. To me, they serve as a reminder that I'm following my divine course.

If you happen upon a feather, pick it up just as you would a found penny or other coin. A feather is sent to you as a message from a loved one who has passed and is now watching over you. Or, to put it another way, feathers appear when angels are near. One might think of them as an angelic business card.

Coins, birds, and feathers are just some of the symbols used by those residing on the other side, reminding us they're around and supporting us. I also believe our loved ones who've crossed over have the ability to show up or reveal themselves as their human loved ones prepare for their own transition home. These types of visitations are common and can occur anytime and anywhere as an individual prepares for this journey. In their book *Final Gifts: Understanding the Special Awareness, Needs, and Communication of the Dying*, authors and former hospice nurses Maggie Callanan and Patricia Kelley share the stories and insights they gathered from their work with the terminally ill. They were witnesses to many occasions where their patients reported sightings of loved ones who crossed over, often indicating these souls were in the room or standing near the bed. The humans who are privy to these visits generally aren't frightened but instead find comfort and joy in these reunions. I believe Mark paid a visit to a certain hospital room, an encounter witnessed by many.

In May 2018, two months after Mark's passing, my eighty-nine-year-old mother-in-law fell in her nursing home room, which resulted in a broken hip. Renie underwent surgical repair of her hip and spent several days recovering in the hospital. Much of this time, as well as the days, weeks, and months prior to her fall, found Renie living in an often blurry and confused state, a symptom of dementia. She often forgot the names and faces of her family, including her own children. Shortly after Mark's passing, we'd attempted to speak with her about our loss, but she either chose not to hear it or honestly couldn't grasp the concept or attach the name to her "bonus" grandson. We later surmised that pieces of this information did make their way into her aged and disease-ridden mind, as, on more than one occasion, she referenced Guy's childhood friend Mark and his untimely passing. It seems she'd confused one Mark with another.

On Mother's Day, many of Renie's children, grandchildren, and great-grandchildren visited with her at the hospital as a way to honor this woman and matriarch who was the foundation of this large and loving family. Stories were told, favorite songs were sung, and laughter filled the room. At one point during this time of reminiscing, Renie looked out into the space in front of her, focusing on no one in particular. Her gaze remained fixed as she spoke about three women who were in her view. None of us could see these women, yet we played along, asking her if she could identify them, which she could not. She also spoke about a beautiful road, and standing in the distance was a young, handsome man. Once again, she couldn't attach a name to the face. The singing and banter resumed but was interrupted as Renie spoke again about the people she saw, including the young man on the road.

At one point, her granddaughter, Renee, asked her if she wanted to go on the road. Renie seemed a bit frightened of this idea and said, "No." Renee asked her if she knew who the young man was, and she shook her head. I happened to be standing at the foot of the bed during this time. I leaned in so Renie could see and hear me more clearly and made sure to identify myself.

"Is the young man Mark?" I asked her.

She said, "Your Mark?"

"Yes, my Mark."

She hesitated for a second. "Yes."

I believe on that Sunday afternoon, my first Mother's Day without my son, Mark showed up, and he wasn't empty-handed. For me, he provided the gift of his presence, and for Renie, he shared a glimpse of the beautiful road that leads to the other side. He allowed her to see that when she was ready to trade this world for another, he and other loved ones who'd traveled this path before would be waiting to guide her home. And Renie made her journey home six days later.

We are grateful for the signs Mark has sent us, reaffirming our belief that he's okay. Five months after Mark's passing, I decided I wanted something more from him than car alarms blaring, lights flickering or randomly turning themselves on, and music flowing from an iPod in the wee hours of the morning. I wanted Mark to speak to me, to tell me things only he and I would know. It was at this time I knew I was ready to take things a step further. It was time to consult with a medium.

Chapter 13
A Medium with a Large Message

If only those left behind on the earth could experience the heightened excitement the newly arrived soul is experiencing, their grief wouldn't be so strong.

—James Van Praagh

Theresa Caputo. John Edward. James Van Praagh. These are the names of three highly recognized mediums or psychics. I learned of James Van Praagh many years ago as I devoured book after book on spirituality. His message, like so many others I was reading at the time, including Deepak Chopra, Dr. Wayne Dyer, Louise Hay, Debbie Shapiro, Eckhart Tolle, Neale Donald Walsch, and

Marianne Williamson, contributed to my spiritual awakening. I'm envious of the special gift that is mediumship; however, as I mentioned, I believe all of us are born with certain psychic abilities or ways to connect with our higher self and others. It just so happens that some have a greater gift or ability to commune with spirit.

Within weeks of Mark's passing, a friend shared the name of a reputable medium who works in my hometown. I stuck this information in a desk drawer and forgot about it. When I made the decision that I was ready for more information regarding Mark and his current comings and goings, I looked up Thomas Windlow via his website. It didn't take long to determine that he was booked for the next six months. Wow! I was anxious to experience a deeper communication with Mark, and it appeared I was going to have to wait a considerable amount of time before this conversation could occur.

I followed the instructions on Thomas's website and scheduled an appointment in March 2019, a very long and distant 180 days in the future. However, by adding your name to a "move forward" list, you gain the ability to snag an appointment should a cancellation occur. I put my name on the list, and less than a month after booking my initial session, I was contacted about an opening on Mr. Windlow's schedule. And so my first ever one-on-one session with a medium occurred about six months after Mark's passing. Not one to risk being late, I gave myself plenty of time to make the drive, arriving in the office parking lot at approximately

11:35 a.m. I include these minute details, as they'd prove to be significant in the opening minutes of my session.

After introducing himself and inviting me to take a seat opposite him at his desk, Thomas began the session, which is recorded on a CD for the client to take home. He began the meeting with a reading of my aura—the energy I brought with me to the appointment. His first words to me are as follows: "You have the hand of God behind your aura. There is also grief showing up in the aura, and it's in layers. You have a younger soul behind you, and then you have a father figure or grandfather figure standing with them. You have so many emotions going on in your aura that you are trying to resolve and solve and fix and rationalize. That is how your aura is showing here."

The first forty-six seconds of a thirty-minute appointment confirmed Mark had joined us for this divine interaction and he wasn't alone. The father figure standing with Mark was his dad and my former husband, Alan. They were joined by my parents, Alois and Hildegard, as well as my maternal grandmother, Franziska. I never had an opportunity to meet my maternal grandmother, as she passed when my mom was a teenager.

Thomas asked for the name of the young soul standing behind me. When I replied, "Mark," he told me Mark had been waiting for over an hour. This first and perhaps most important revelation on that Tuesday afternoon was that Mark had shown up, and not only was he right on time, but he'd arrived early. Yes, that boy still carries his astute sense of timeliness even on the other side. Thomas had an earlier in-person session with a woman around 11:30 a.m., the time approximating my arrival in the parking lot. Mark kept coming through to Thomas during that session, which prompted him at one point to pause and ask the client who Mark was. She replied that she didn't know a Mark, after which Thomas dismissed him, since in his words, "I do not like to talk to souls I don't know."

It's a good thing Thomas records these sessions, as there is so much information that gets relayed back and forth. Some of the key points from my first meeting are as follows:

Thomas informed me several times during my appointment there was no turmoil in Mark's passing. In his words, "Mark walked out of his body with ease. He did not suffer, and his light center was whole when it left. Energetically, his soul mission was done. He did go into the light."

As I've mentioned, I believe when it's our time to cross over, we are aided in this journey by loved ones who have gone before us. Thomas shared three times during our time together that Alan had helped his son cross over.

Thomas confirmed Mark is an old soul, and he mentioned more than once that "Mark is a good kid." He made a reference to Mark's loyalty, a quality I was familiar with. "Mark was extremely loyal while here on Earth, and he remains loyal to these friendships." He also mentioned that Mark is a kind soul and he will finish his education in heaven. Thomas asked about Mark's major, and when I shared he'd been studying psychology, he replied, "Mark would have been a great psychologist. He has therapeutic ears."

For any skeptics who might be questioning the legitimacy of mediums and their ability to connect with souls who've crossed over, I offer two examples from my appointment where Thomas shared things with me that would never have been known to him. Early in my session, he asked me about a "hand plate with a finger on it that was bluish in color." He said it was some sort of print or artwork from Mark's childhood. It took me a few seconds to wrack my brain, but I was finally able to make sense of what Mark showed him. Just days before this appointment, I'd been going through a large plastic tub where I kept artwork from Mark's school years. Near the bottom of the tub were a few things he'd made while attending preschool. Among these items was a Mother's Day present, an oven mitt he'd given me that year. On one side, Mark had made an imprint of his tiny hands using paint. His name was written on one hand, and the other had the words, "Mother's Tea 2001." On the back side were more handprints and the words, "Mommy's Helping Hands." This was the hand plate Mark showed Thomas. I'd held it in my hands the day before the appointment.

Thomas asked me if Mark had been texting my phone or manipulating any electronic devices, as he confirmed spirits are capable of performing such tasks with ease. I told him about the incidents involving the alarm in Mark's car. When I finished, Thomas said he heard Mark chuckle, a guilty laugh.

Toward the end of my session, Thomas took a final, sweeping glance of the room and shared the following: "I've got to tell you, when I look at your mom's and dad's energy and Mark's energy, there is no comparison. Your parents' light offers no comparison to the soft light that Mark is carrying." This statement was no surprise to me. My parents remained in my life well into adulthood. As I grew older and more spiritually aware, I often felt more like their teacher and less like their student. I believe the opposite can be said for the time I spent with my son. Mark is most likely an older soul than me, and I was more his student and less his teacher.

One of the last things Thomas shared with me that day in regard to Mark was this statement: "Celebrate his life, and don't celebrate with sadness. Mark did not die. Nothing dies. We merely change form. We move."

I've had two additional sessions with Thomas in the time since our initial meeting. Mark has continued to show up and has always been accompanied by his dad, my parents, and at least one of my grandmothers. It appears Mark is the group's designated speaker, as he does most if not all of the communicating. Alan and the others have offered a "hello" but otherwise remain present in their silence. I'm grateful to all of them for showing up and for recognizing it's Mark I most want to hear from. And it seems Mark knows this, as he always shares a few tidbits that are personal in nature and couldn't otherwise be known to Thomas. Mark lets me know he's doing well. In the time immediately following one of these sessions, my mood is lifted and I feel a certain kind of peace come over me. I wish I could share that this shifting of perceptions is long lived. However, that isn't the case. Within a day or so, my familiar and burdensome feelings of loss, sadness, and despair return. I'm grateful for the respite despite its brevity, as it provides me with a chance to catch my breath before once again strapping on the leaden and cumbersome pack that is grief.

My journey of grief isn't over, and it seems likely I will walk this path for some time to come. The religion of joan has provided me with the tools necessary to navigate my way through the unknown, and birds, namely a male cardinal and a momma hawk, have flown alongside me, providing me with inspiration, hope, and strength. I'm also grateful for pennies from heaven, blaring car alarms, and messages from a medium that confirm, at least for me, our loved ones who have crossed over are never far away. With that said, grief is hard work, and one must often dig deep to unearth the skills necessary to come to some sort of terms with our loss.

Part 4

The Tigger Effect

Promise me you'll always remember: You're braver than you believe, and stronger than you seem, and smarter than you think.

—A. A. Milne, creator of
Winnie the Pooh (and Tigger too)

chapter 14
Resilience

Out of suffering have emerged the strongest souls; the most massive characters are seared with scars.

—Kahlil Gibran

Soldier. Fighter. Warrior. These terms are most often used to describe individuals who serve in the military. However, they can also be used to describe people who are battling cancer and other life-threatening or life-altering diseases as well as those working diligently for human rights and other social causes. The term "warrior" is currently used in pop culture and on social media sites in regard to women. One dictionary definition states, "Today, the word warrior is frequently used to describe a person who is very strong and doesn't give up easily." I would also include the term "resilient" when describing such an individual.

What is resilience? According to the American Psychological Association, "Resilience is the process of adapting well in the face of adversity, trauma, tragedy, threats, or significant sources of stress—such as family and relationship problems, serious health issues or workplace and financial stressors. It means 'bouncing back' from difficult experiences." In researching her book *The Gifts of Imperfection—Let Go of Who You Think You're Supposed to Be and Embrace Who You Are,* author Brené Brown found that resilience was also tied to spirit or one's spirituality. I read Ms. Brown's book long after I began my own soul-searching spiritual quest, and her words confirm many tenets of the religion of joan, especially in regard to the concept that we all are one. And love acts as the cord that connects us. I think the "s" in resilience stands for spirit.

I believe each and every one of us is gifted with the capacity for resilience; however, like its sister attributes, compassion and empathy, we must hone these God-given skills throughout our lifetime. Some of us may never need to call upon resilience to guide us through rough or troubling times, but it's a good idea to keep this tool sharpened and ready to go should the need arise. Think of it like your auto or home insurance policy—you invest in them despite the fact you may never need to use them. I came across a list of characteristics possessed by the resilient as outlined in an article by K. M. Connor:

- Internal locus of control
- Strong self-esteem, self-efficiency
- Have personal goals
- Sense of meaningfulness
- Can use past successes to confront current challenges
- Can view stress as a challenge/way to get stronger
- Use humor, patience, tolerance, and optimism
- Can adapt to change
- Action-oriented approach
- Have strong relationships and ask for help
- Have faith

As I peruse this list in relation to myself and my story, I believe I can check off many or most of these items, save for the attribute of patience and the ability to adapt to change. I have never and would never claim patience as one of my virtues. I've had to count to ten or twenty or one hundred many times when dealing with certain situations and/or individuals, and this usually does nothing to increase my degree of patience. It merely reaffirms my ability to count. And as far as adapting to change is concerned, I believe we all arrive on this planet with the ability to go with the flow. Children offer the best examples of our innate ability to remain flexible and malleable as we're confronted with life's twists and turns. As we morph from child to adult, many of us appear to lose our ability to yield to change, instead becoming set in our ways, preferring to stick with the status quo even if that proves to be nonproductive or no longer useful or self-serving. Change is something we fear rather than embrace. Tenet number six of the religion of joan reminds us when we're living in the presence of fear, we are existing in a place devoid of love.

It appears I surrendered to fear at a rather young age. When I was sixteen, as part of a high school English class assignment, I wrote two sentences that pretty much summed up my feelings about change: "When Mr. or Mrs. Change comes knocking at my door, I rarely answer it. I pretend it's another door-to-door salesman just trying to sell me something I don't want." My teacher had apparently done the same, according to the two-word comment she scribbled on my paper with her little red pen—"Me too."

Ms. Connor's list of characteristics suggests these attributes might also be the definition of someone who isn't only resilient but also fulfilled, driven, faithful, and prone to many moments of joy and contentment.

I believe the last item on Connor's list confirms the notion that the "s" in resilience really does come from spirit. If you have faith, which can be something different for everyone, you believe in something greater than yourself and trust this "something greater" has your back. We possess a certain amount of free will as we move through life, checking off boxes that aid in our growth and evolution; however, we're often redirected toward a path where we can achieve our highest potential. As life tests and pushes and challenges you, it's often faith that guides you as you work through and process your situation and arrive at a place of acceptance. And this work is often solitary, as there's simply no one else—parent, spouse, friend, neighbor, coworker, or child—who can do this work for us. I think Mary Holloway sums this up best: "Resilience is knowing that you are the only one that has the power and responsibility to pick yourself up."

As I pondered the concept of resilience, it occurred to me that the words "resilient" and "resistant" are strikingly similar. Each word contains nine letters, and six of these letters occupy the same place within the word:

RESILIENT

RESISTANT

This is where their similarity ends, especially when one uses them in reference to change. Resilience implies a go-with-the-flow mentality, a certain fluidity like that of a river flowing freely within its banks. Resistance, on the other hand, suggests a sort of standing in place, a situation that can result in stagnancy. Resistance is the dam holding one back from forward progress, which can result in becoming stuck. I don't know about you, but I prefer the freeing feeling of fluidity over the heaviness and permanence of being cemented in place. It seems possible resilience arises from an inner strength residing deep within most of us, if not all of us. We might not be aware of its existence until we find ourselves faced with challenging situations or events.

The words "strong" or "stronger" are used three times in Ms. Connor's list. We often think of strength in the physical sense, such as bulging biceps or the ability to lift heavy objects, which is also probably why men are frequently thought of as the stronger of the two sexes. There might be some truth in a man's ability to beat most women in an arm wrestling match or bench press competition; however, this is largely attributable to the design of the male body and its greater abundance of the hormone testosterone. I believe I've been gifted with a certain amount of strength via my German DNA and my Leo the Lion astrological sign, but I also believe mental strength, or inner strength, has little to do with genetics, body type, hormones, or the stars and is equally available to both genders. Former professional football player and wrestler Alex Karras says this best: "Toughness is in the soul and spirit, not in muscles."

And to further drive this point home, the Dalai Lama sums it up this way: "When we meet real tragedy in life, we can react in two ways, either by losing hope and falling into self-destructive habits, or by using the challenge to find our inner strength."

When it comes to finding strength and resilience in regard to the loss of a loved one, especially a child, the journey of grief is unique, personal, and often lonely. It can also be messy and confusing and most certainly isn't linear. There's no real right or wrong way to travel this path; however, the ultimate goal is to achieve some sort of acceptance. And, for the record, acceptance is never synonymous with forgetting. A cherished loved one who's crossed over can't be forgotten. It's simply impossible. For me, arriving at a place of acceptance indicates I've come to terms with my loss. I acknowledge the fact I'm still here; therefore, my life still has some sort of purpose. I might not know exactly what that purpose is or what it looks like, but I must rise each day and find my way.

In the days, weeks, and months since Mark's passing, I've never attended a support group or buried my nose in books about grief. And although I'm a huge believer in counseling, I have yet to seek the guidance of a licensed therapist. None of those seem necessary, at least not at this time. I allow my tears to flow easily and daily as a way to heal. I believe my eyes are windows to my soul's struggles, and by allowing their wells to drain onto a tissue or sleeve or whatever is handy, I'm ridding my body of grief in a healthy manner. I've also used writing as a means to express my topsy-turvy feelings and emotions. Tears can exit the body via words, and these droplets of grief can be captured on paper.

Thomas, the medium, confirmed that I'm not alone in my grief. When I entered his office for my first session, he shared that the hand of God was with me. He let me know I'm being carried.

And there's even more good news. Cultivating mental fortitude doesn't have to be a solo endeavor, as there can also be strength in numbers. Ms. Connor suggests that having strong relationships contributes to the ability for resiliency. It's always helpful to have a few family members, friends, and/or confidantes who can offer love and support when we experience difficult or challenging times. These folks often know how to listen and refrain from offering unsolicited advice. If you're fortunate, these individuals might also get where you're coming from, and as a huge bonus, they might also be practiced in our innate ability for empathy. I do believe there's strength in numbers. I'm a card-carrying member of a select group of women that began its formation well before Mark's passing. Before you get all excited and perhaps even a bit jealous, this is a selective and somewhat secret club, one no member voluntarily signed up for.

chapter 15
The Club

Some people, as far as your senses are concerned, just feel like home.

—High Fidelity

There are many clubs or organizations where people can come together to share a common interest, provide support to one another, and gather for recreation. A few examples that come to mind are bowling leagues, support groups, community service organizations, and book clubs. Membership might involve paying dues or committing to a specific number of hours per week in order to belong and might even require some sort of vetting or application process prior to joining.

With the passing of my son, I became a card-carrying member of the Club No Mother Wants to Join. I unwillingly united with women all over the world who've experienced the horror that is child loss. It became apparent to me long before Mark passed away that within the confines of my somewhat small world, I crossed paths with many women who'd lost a child. On more than one occasion, I made a conscious mental note of this reality and took the time to ponder this somewhat odd and strange phenomenon. Why did I know so many mothers who had buried a child? I'd become acquainted with them at work, via a writing group, through my neighborhood and local schools, and by literally bumping into one in a divine encounter at the local Walmart. Since I don't believe in chance, luck, or accidents, I knew my connection to these ladies had some greater meaning. This particular mystery was solved in March 2018. I'd been connected with these women by something more than just the workplace or neighborhood. Together, we share a trauma of epic proportions that is morose, tragic, and somewhat beyond comprehension, and we provide living proof that the unthinkable can and does happen to people. To good people.

There are eleven women in the group, which now includes me, their newest member. Six of the ladies live within my zip code. Yes, you read that correctly. Another member lives in the area, and three live outside my home state. Of this elite eleven, only myself and one other mother lost our only biological child, a son. Here are a few other notes about the children and mothers:

- Of the eleven children who passed, two are females and nine are males.
- Seven succumbed to illness. Cancer was the snatcher of four lives. One lost a lifetime battle with granulomatosis with polyangiitis (GPA), formerly known as Wegener's. One passed from complications associated with mitochondrial disease. Mark was lost to diabetes.
- Five of them left Earth unexpectedly like Mark. One was the victim of a car crash, one passed from an overdose, one drowned, and one passed as the result of accidental strangulation.
- One member lost her daughter nearly twenty years ago, but for a few like me, our loss is much more recent.
- The time spent on Earth by these treasured souls ranged from seven years to just over two decades.

The names and ages of these beautiful spirits are as follows—girls followed by the boys:

Kelsey (16)
Natalie (18)

Arun (11)
Blaine (22)
Brody (7)
Grey (16)
Isaac (17)
Jeffrey (12)
Mark H. (20)
Mark (18)
Tim (19)

The women in the Club No Mother Wants to Join are individual and unique, and so, too, is their journey of grief. I'm not privy to all of the tools these women have yanked out of their toolbox, though I know about half have used faith as a way to cope and make sense of their loss. Some have attended grief support groups. The vast majority have arrived at some place of peace and acceptance regarding their loss. They've made a concerted effort to heal; however, according to Thomas, the medium, "A parent can never fully heal the loss of a child." I believe he's 100 percent correct. We will in many ways mourn the loss of our child until we take our last breath. By the way, most of these mothers shared this experience with a spouse and other children who were forced to travel this heartbreaking path. Fathers and siblings aren't excluded from the club. I speak solely about the mothers, as they're the ones I've come to know personally.

In the days and weeks after Mark's passing, I was contacted by or connected with each one of the ladies, and I'm grateful for their kind, supportive words and open arms. I've spent the most time in the company of the eldest member of the group. Dauna lost her daughter nearly twenty years ago, so she has the most time and perspective in regard to traversing her own grief journey. She assures me it does get better; however, whenever we share stories about our kids, including the funny and poignant ones, it is obvious she still misses her precious daughter. And when I reveal my deeply personal emotions, especially my anger and bewilderment in regard to Mark's passing, she often shares the insight she gained when faced with similar feelings. Her validation reassures me I'm not crazy or losing it. But most of all, Dauna provides me with living proof one can still find purpose and joy in life despite experiencing tremendous loss, which now also includes the passing of her husband. At the age of seventy-two, this socially active mother, grandmother, and former educator is a part-time caregiver to an aging parent, maintains a household, is a published writer and gifted speaker, and mentors student teachers at a local university. Dauna has found a way to march forward and make the most of her remaining days. She, like Tigger, has bounced back.

As part of the work that is grief, I've found a sense of healing and purpose in ensuring Mark's memory lives on. I want to continue to provide proof he existed and that his brief life impacted others in a positive and meaningful way. When settling on a name for our one and only child, Alan and I could not have known that the name we chose would also come to define the life of this special soul. Mark left a mark on many.

Part 5

There's Nothing Wrong with Writing

Write what should not be forgotten.

—Isabel Allende

chapter 16
Mark, My Words

Strive to always spread kindness and empathy towards others.

—Mark J. Hyams, age 18

Schools use writing as a means to expand and reinforce the vocabulary of children. Students are often encouraged to jot down stories about their family, friends, and pets as a means of learning sentence structure and expression. Often, the kids also include illustrations alongside their words as a way to add detail to the story. In early elementary school, Mark and his fellow classmates published their stories within the pages of small booklets made from folded pieces of paper. Mark crafted many of these mini books, and nestled within the pages were his simple yet revealing words.

I kept many of these treasured writings and spent time going through them after Mark passed. I noticed an evolution in his writing that was indicative of his growth and ever-expanding vocabulary. As Mark entered sixth grade, his words took on a more mature and introspective tone, which was now shared in the form of essays and short stories. These writing assignments became more prevalent as he progressed through school, not only in English class but also as research assignments in other subjects, such as science and social studies. Mark's earliest samples completed in kindergarten through second grade include poems, such as this one:

> "Mark"
> There once was a boy named Mark,
> He loved to go to the park,
> He jumped up and down,
> And ran all around,
> Until he got hit by some bark!

Here's another about our Rottweiler, written and illustrated at age five:

> "Fritz"
> My dog, Fritz,
> Doesn't like to sit
> He does like the car
> And he likes to go far
> In the summer we take him to the pool

Where he thinks he's real cool
When we take him to The Cone
He gets an ice cream of his own
He likes to go to the mall
Where he usually has a ball
And that's all

Later, his jottings began to display more depth and awareness, such as this sample:

> "The Colors of Life"
> Green is the color of spring,
> That makes the birds sing.
> Yellow is the color of light,
> When the birds take flight.
> Blue is the color of the clouds,
> When the clouds sigh.

And Mark's "List of Beliefs":

> I believe in never judging a book by its cover.
> I believe that living with a chronic illness won't keep me from achieving my fullest potential.
> I believe practice makes you better.
> I believe everyone makes mistakes.
> I believe everyone has a purpose in life.
> I believe everything bad will pass.

As Mark moved from elementary to junior high and high school, writing assignments became more complex. In the summer between his junior and senior year, Mark's school offered a week-long class designed to provide students with assistance in writing the common app essay, a requirement of some colleges and universities as part of their application process. The two schools Mark intended to apply to—Miami University in Oxford, Ohio, and the University of Cincinnati—required this writing sample. If you're unfamiliar with the common app essay, there are a few rules associated with the process. Applicants are provided five prompts, choosing one that resonates with them, which becomes their topic for the maximum 650-word submission. On the first day of the summer class, Mark's teacher provided the five prompts that were being used for the 2015/2016 common app essays. Mark chose prompt number five: "Discuss an accomplishment or event, formal or informal, that marked your transition from childhood to adulthood within your culture, community, or family."

Mark chose to write about his part-time job at Reebok, a store at the local outlet mall. Mark had been hired as a sales associate in the spring of 2015. In this new position, Mark was expected to greet and assist customers. For a seventeen-year-old introvert, striking up conversations with strangers isn't the easiest of tasks. As Mark revealed in his stunningly personal and candid essay, his part-time job provided him with much more than pocket change. Here's his submission in its entirety:

"Hi, welcome to Reebok" I say with a warm smile on my face. "How are you today?" I also usually add, "Is there anything I can help you with?" as I cross my fingers hoping the customer mouths the word "yes." This simple interaction with our patrons is why I have fallen in love with my retail job. I didn't always cherish the idea of talking to everyone I came into contact with. From the moment I was born, I had been attached to my mother's leg—literally. I was the kid who never played at recess. The kid who ate lunch by himself. The kid who never spoke in class. I would just observe and listen intently. (Supposedly, I inherited my dad's quiet, somewhat introverted personality and not my mother's extroverted one.) I don't regret the decision I made to stay to myself. I only regret all of the missed conversation opportunities.

The concept of initiating a conversation sparked a fear inside me equivalent to being sentenced to a lifetime in prison. Fortunately, it was easy to avoid starting a conversation with others but being able to hold a conversation when I was spoken to was another issue. I would often just hope that people would not acknowledge me at all and I could remain "invisible." However, when I was spoken to, I minded my manners and responded with a simple answer. This strategy, to my surprise, did not always work, as I learned each year on the first day of school. The scenario remained the same. "Hello everyone. Form a circle, state your name and share one thing about yourself," said the teacher. My heart pounded faster and faster as the spotlight of attention grew closer. "My name is Mark and I." By this point, my face was sunburn red and I am trembling with fear about what to say. As the torturing ended and I gave my answer, a little part of me grew inside, though I can't say that I was fully aware this transformation was going on. My answer may have changed each year, along with the teacher, classroom and classmates, but the ritual remained the same. And so did my fear to some degree.

I have been at my retail job for about three months, and in that short time, I have learned a new way to engage people. Sharing something about myself doesn't have to mean verbally reciting something personal. It can be as simple as a friendly "hello," or listening to someone's story. Through my amazing interactions with people at Reebok, I get a chance to learn things about others that I would have never known. This might include hearing about events in a coworker's life, or a conversation with a male customer about how his spouse managed to drag him to virtually every store in the mall. With each person who walks through the crystal clear double doors, I embrace the opportunity to share something about myself without ever really telling them about myself. By appreciating the customer, I tell them all they need to know about me—I listen and I care. Reflecting back on my childhood, being quiet and somewhat introverted has not done my true personality justice. I had not been sharing a part of myself that I wish others could have seen.

Growing up, my mother always told me that when my father was alive, he had the ability to talk to anyone. I always thought, well I'm not my father. As I have grown older, each social barrier I once put up in my life gets knocked down. New barriers

> might arise, however, I will continue to embrace new challenges in my life and strive to be like the man, my dad, I never got to know. I will become the man that I wish he could see.

Upon reading this essay, it became apparent to me that Mark was beginning to reveal the inner workings of his mind. He was using the written word as a way of sharing deeply personal thoughts about all he had lost. It should be noted that in the time shortly after Alan's passing, I never sought counseling or grief support for either Mark or myself. I attribute this to a few factors. First, we moved from Texas to Ohio two months after Alan passed, so I was otherwise occupied with packing, unpacking, and settling into our new home and community. Second, Mark was quite young, and I wasn't sure how much he would have benefitted from therapy. And lastly, I was in denial—denial about Alan's illness, his passing, my anger, and, most importantly, my grief. In the fall of 2003, after I completed my chemotherapy treatments, Mark and I attended bimonthly meetings with Fernside, a local grief support group for children. Mark spent time with kids his age who'd also suffered parent loss. The facilitators used art projects as a means to encourage the kids to express themselves. I attended my own meeting comprised of men and women also grieving the loss of a spouse or partner.

Not long after Mark's type 1 diabetes diagnosis, I decided to seek out the services of a licensed counselor. In the days and weeks after his diagnosis, Mark became more vocal about all that had transpired in his short life, and I was hopeful he might share any unexpressed grief or questions with a therapist. Mark did more art therapy with his psychologist, but in the end, he revealed little to her. Since Mark was slow to warm up to strangers, it seems possible he wasn't provided enough time to become comfortable and trusting with Dr. Vivian. One day, as Mark and I hung out in the great room, he asked me questions about his dad and other topics. I quickly realized I was witnessing a breakthrough of sorts, so I wrote the questions down in a little booklet I crafted from folded copy paper just like the ones Mark made in elementary school.

The first question he asked was, "When am I (Joan) going to marry someone?" At this time in our life, Alan had been gone for about four years, and, as mentioned earlier, I had little time, desire, or inclination for dating. I was curious as to why Mark asked me about marriage, so I answered his question with a question: "Why do you think I should get married?" His immediate response was somewhat simple yet practical: "It would be easier. There'd be someone to watch me when you (Mom) are at school." In the spring of 2005, I'd applied for and was accepted into a local university's master's program in community counseling, where I intended to fulfill a long-time goal of becoming a licensed counselor. I have a B.A. in psychology with a minor in sociology. I completed my first class that summer and was enrolled in two classes for the fall semester. Mark's diabetes diagnosis came two weeks before the start of the new school year. I was overwhelmed by all I had to learn in order to care for Mark and knew it would take me a while to grasp the tedious and often cumbersome routine that is diabetes care. It was at this time I chose to withdraw from the university, stifling my pursuit of a graduate degree.

I viewed Mark's initial question and response as yet another example of his very practical and logical side as well as wisdom far beyond his seven years. When I shared this story with his therapist, she concluded that Mark was looking for normalcy as well as someone who'd take care of him should something happen to me. Mark asked another question that day, one that offered a glimpse inside the mind of a boy living life without his father. However, before I share more of our conversation, it's necessary for me to provide a little backstory.

Once Mark gained the ability for speech, he always referred to Alan and me as Dad and Mom. Sometime after Alan's passing, Mark began referring to his late father by his first name. Despite my limited background in psychology, I knew enough to conclude that by using his dad's first name, Mark unconsciously exhibited a form of avoidance or detachment. Later on, he also began to call me Joan rather than Mom or Mommy, something he would continue to do well into his preteen years. His therapist did confirm that by using our first names, Mark was protecting himself. He knew his father was gone, and even though he wasn't privy to all of the details of my bout with cancer, he knew enough to understand it was serious. If something happened to me, Mark might somehow come to terms with the loss of Joan and Alan, not Mom and Dad. I never really challenged or pressured Mark to refer to me as Mom. Instead, I chose to pick my battles, and this one wasn't worth fighting. I would occasionally gently remind him he was my only child and the only person on the planet who could call me Mom. In junior high, some of Mark's friends teased him when they overheard him refer to me as Joan. Perhaps it was this form of peer pressure that enabled Mark to once again call me Mom, or maybe enough time had passed and the fear of losing me had waned.

In 2005, as Mark and I continued our impromptu conversation, he also asked me the following: "When is Alan going to come alive again? Can I see him for one day? I just want him back." Wow! I vividly recall being somewhat blindsided by these questions. How long had this boy been holding on to hope his dad might reappear in his life? A few hours after Alan passed away, Mark and I were up in his room, getting him dressed for the day, as a neighbor had invited him to join her and her two boys for an afternoon at the park. Mark had been his usual quiet and observant self for most of the morning as I spent time on the phone, making travel arrangements and finalizing funeral plans. He probably spent some of this time processing the news of his father's passing, at least as much as the underdeveloped and inexperienced mind of a three-year-old could conceive. That afternoon, as we worked to get him clothed, I began a conversation. I told Mark his dad was in heaven and was no longer in pain. I also told him his dad could now walk normally, so he no longer needed crutches, a walker, or a wheelchair. Mark's immediate response to this information was, "Since he's all better, can he come back?" I admit I was somewhat stunned and taken off guard by his matter-of-fact question, an observation provided by a toddler that was intelligent, logical, and naive. I responded by calmly and gently informing him it didn't work that way. I let him know Daddy was unable to return, as his place was now in heaven. Looking back, it seems possible my explanation didn't provide Mark with all of the answers he was searching for, and as time passed, he'd held out some kind of hope Alan would return. Four years later, when the question was asked again, I didn't rush into some practical explanation of Alan's inability to return, but I chose to ask Mark what he'd do if he had one more day. As Mark proceeded to share his plans, it became apparent this visit would require more than twenty-four hours.

First, he wanted to spend time at home just talking, father and son. He would then take his dad on a tour of our home, which included spending time in his bedroom. They would snap a few photos for posterity. After that, father and son would take a walk with Fritz, Alan's beloved Rottweiler, who was still alive and doing fairly well despite being ten years old. For lunch, they'd share a meal at Bravo, one of Mark's favorite restaurants, where he always ordered the spaghetti with marinara sauce sans meat and the garlic mashed potatoes. He also wanted Alan to join him on a mini trip to Hocking Hills for some time spent hiking among nature. Alas, so much to do with so little time. Mark let me know when it came time for Alan to leave again, he would be sad.

This impromptu conversation provided me with much insight and information into the mind of my fatherless boy. It was on that day, within the safe and familiar comforts of home, Mark decided to open up and reveal some of the inner workings of his deep-thinking mind. And I was his audience of one. As Mark made his way through his tween and teen years, he continued to surprise me with his old-soul insights and observations. Much of this was done via conversation; however, some was revealed through writing.

Fast-forward to the predawn hours of December 26, 2015. Three boys, two of whom were brothers, were traveling in a car when the driver lost control, striking a light pole and crashing into a tree. Only two boys made it out unharmed and alive. The passenger who didn't survive was named Mark, and he was well known to us. The two Marks, who were the same age, had crossed paths in elementary school and had hung around together for a brief period of time.

In April 2016, I received notice of a $1,000 scholarship the family created in honor and memory of their Mark, who'd been on track to graduate from high school just months after his passing. The requirements for applying for this award were to submit an essay (minimum of one thousand words) about the power of friendship, including a discussion of one or more suggested prompts. The deadline was Monday, May 9, 2016, a date I remember well. I shared the contest information with Mark and conveyed my strong desire for him to participate in some way. It didn't matter to me if he wrote an essay or not, as the motive wasn't to win the contest and collect the scholarship money. I suggested he write a letter to the family, acknowledging their loss.

At the time of the contest announcement, Mark was in the final weeks of his senior year. He'd chosen a rigorous academic schedule for his final year of school. He was knee-deep in homework, papers, and test preparation as well as working about twenty hours a week at Reebok and fulfilling his weekly community service commitment. As the deadline crept closer and closer, I kept reminding Mark about participating in the project that honored his former childhood friend. He would later tell me my words, "Write a letter to the family," sparked an idea for what would become his unconventional submission.

On May 9, the deadline date for the contest, I came home from work and found Mark holed up in his room. I assumed he was chipping away at homework before leaving for his weekly volunteer gig. At about 5:30 p.m., his bedroom door flew open, and Mark met me in the great room on his way out the door. He thrust a few sheets of paper into my hand, informing me he'd completed the scholarship contest essay and asking me to get it to the family. I thanked him for getting it done and agreed to drop it off at their house. Out the door he went as I sat down to read what he'd written.

Attached to the completed, two-page application form were seven pieces of paper. Mark had written five different letters. Instead of submitting a conventional essay, he'd chosen to offer his thoughts on friendship in a creative and unique way. There were three somewhat brief letters addressed to Mark, the honoree of this contest, as well as two letters addressed to his family. The final and by far the longest letter was written by Mark to his future self. It's this letter I choose to share. Oh, and Mark won the contest.

> Dear Future Me,
>
> It wasn't until I learned of the untimely passing of a former friend that I began to realize the importance of even the shortest friendships. Why should I have to wait until it is too late to share a memory with an old friend or acquaintance? Why can't I take the time out of my day to catch up with the people around me? Whether it's my family, friends, neighbors, or former teachers, there is always room to remember those who positively influenced my childhood. I once watched a TED talk about the key to happiness. The simple answer was to maintain healthy relationships with those around you. Instead of pursuing the next

must-have thing, or gather material possessions, why don't I look to those around me? I can sit down at the dinner table with my mom and have a lasting conversation, or maybe text an old school friend and see how he or she is doing.

If the passing of Mark has taught me one thing, it is to cherish every moment I spend with others. No matter if I like them at the moment or not, there is always something I can learn from everyone I bump into on my earthly journey. Life is too short and unpredictable to procrastinate. Instead of being my usual quiet self, why not open up to people and see where it takes me? The worst thing that can happen is we can pass by each other, or, if I am lucky, it might take me down a path similar to the one that Mark introduced me to. All of my friends, family, and even those I've bumped into during life have shaped me in some way. Sometimes for the better, others for the worse, but overall each was a unique experience nonetheless. Life is too precious to stay to myself, so strive to always spread kindness and empathy towards others. I hope that one day, wherever you are, you stop to reflect on which relationships you choose to start and which ones you may have passed. I hope that you come to realize the importance of everyone in your life before the clock runs out of time. I do this in the loving memory of Mark and all of those who have touched my life in some way.

Love,
Mark Hyams

Knowing what I know now, that my own precious Mark would leave this earth just over twenty-six months later, I find the second to last sentence in this note to self somewhat eerily prophetic: "I hope that you come to realize the importance of everyone in your life before the clock runs out of time." Mark Hyams's clock would run out of time sometime in the late morning or early afternoon of Tuesday, March 6, 2018. And this wasn't the only prophetic glimpse into the future he'd penned. I happened upon a list of wishes Mark had written as a first grader. In his booklet "I Wish," page three offered this request: "I wish I was twenty years old." What six-year-old pens the words, "I wish I was twenty"? Boys of that age are more inclined to jot down a wish list that includes toys, video games, special treats, or perhaps a Disney vacation. And why did Mark pick that particular age? Did his spirit reveal a secret to human Mark? As previously noted, Mark left this earth just weeks after his twentieth birthday.

If you recall, my obstetrician calculated Mark's arrival date as sometime in early March. I was going through Mark's baby book recently, looking for some information. As I thumbed through, I came upon his actual due date: March 6, 1998. Mark wasn't born on that date, but exactly twenty years later, he left this Earth. I was stunned when I saw this, as I didn't remember it at all. In my mind, there's something prophetic about this date as it relates to Mark's most recent incarnation.

Not long after Mark's passing, an article was written about him in the student newspaper at Miami University. A few of Mark's friends were interviewed for the piece. It was here we learned about Mark's dedication to his small circle of friends. Apparently, his dorm room was a favorite gaming hangout, and Mark was the host with the most. He tried to make everyone comfortable in the snug and confining space and also provided snacks to ward off late-night munchies. One friend memorialized Mark with this statement: "What I remember most about Mark is that, honestly, he cared."

The Miami Student article also revealed that on occasion Mark played the role of counselor, a fitting title for a young man whose major was psychology. It seems obvious that Mark's ISFJ attributes, those traits that indicate an extreme sensitivity and loyalty, would come to define him as a trusted and devoted friend as well as a decent human being. As his mom, I knew he was special. This isn't merely the observation of a proud mother but rather an affirmation of my belief that old souls, the ones who've traveled here for many, many lifetimes, are a gift. Their light is bright, their vibration is strong, and their love is limitless.

I'll end this chapter with further proof Mark lived a somewhat selfless life and his dedication and devotion to others often meant putting their needs ahead of his own. During the summer of 2008, Mark, then age ten, attended a day camp in our area, as he was too young to stay home alone while I worked. The camp provided bus service for those who didn't live within close proximity. Each morning and afternoon, I dropped Mark off and then picked him up from a bus stop not too far from my place of employment. During the afternoon ride home, I always asked him about his day. During one such conversation, he told me he and his fellow campers had played a game where everyone made one wish that was then shared with the group. Mark proceeded to ask me, "If you had one wish, what would it be?" I embarrassingly recall that for a smattering of seconds, my mind wandered to materialistic and mundane items like money, a new car, and a larger home. Fortunately, I quickly snapped out of this shallow trance, and my thoughts turned to the one thing I wished for above all else. I told him I wished for a cure for type 1 diabetes. Mark replied instantly, "No, Joan, you don't want a cure for type 1 diabetes. You want a cure for cancer, which kills far more people."

My young son, the one who stuck his fingers with needles and had to take a shot every time he ate, wasn't focused on himself and the horrible disease he lived with every day. He was concerned about others and their suffering. And he knew all of this at the tender age of ten. I believe a quote by Abraham Lincoln describes and summarizes the time Mark Johann Hyams spent on this planet:

> "In the end, it's not the years in your life
> that count. It's the life in your years."

chapter 17
What Might Have Been

*There is no friendship, no love, like that
of the parent for the child.*

—Henry Ward Beecher

In the winter of 2004, after I'd completed my intravenous chemotherapy treatments, I enrolled in a creative writing course at a suburban branch of the university Mark would attend years later. At the end of each class, the instructor provided us with a writing assignment to complete during the week. During our next scheduled meeting, we could volunteer to share our work with the group, who would then offer comments and critiques. I often wrote about cancer, a topic I knew plenty about as both a patient and caregiver and one that was on the forefront of my mind since I was still in treatment. I also often wrote about loss—the loss of a spouse and the loss of a "normal" family life. One assignment resulted in the following piece entitled "What Might Have Been," which is written from Mark's perspective.

> It came knocking on our door one sweltering August day when I was just six months old. I wish he had never answered the door, as we had a lifetime of things to do together as father and son. We would walk hand in hand to the park where I would beg him to push me on the swing "just one more time." We would go to McDonald's and eat French fries and chug chocolate milk shakes, eschewing the hamburgers—he for religious reasons and me because Mom is a vegetarian.
>
> In the summertime, we'd play a game of catch in the backyard, or watch the pros play at the stadium downtown. We would take a family vacation to the place where Mickey lives or travel east to the state of his birth. We would visit Brooklyn, Long Island, and take in the sights and sounds of the city that never sleeps. In the wintertime,

we would dare to take on the white, icy hills on our two-man sled. We'd shriek as we raced to the bottom, snow spraying our red, chapped faces. Afterwards, I'd help him dig out the driveway, and then together we would build a man of snow.

In the evenings and on weekends, we would scour his bottomless CD collection and make our selections. We'd blast the stereo, singing and dancing to the music of his youth—Chuck Berry, Elvis, the Beatles. He would know all of the words. (I've been told he could've been a winning contestant on *Name That Tune* if such a show existed in the late 1990s.) At bedtime, he would tuck me in and together we'd share his passion for the printed word. In the early years, we would read Winnie the Pooh and Dr. Seuss and later, the Hardy Boys and Harry Potter.

He would teach me how to ride a bike, chasing after me down the street shouting, "Keep on pedaling." We would watch TV together— The Discovery Channel, Animal Planet, and ESPN—slumped like lumps on the sofa, feet-to-feet. We would experience "my firsts" together—first day of school, first visit from the tooth fairy, first goal at soccer, first school dance. He'd be proud of me dressed in my cap and gown. I would be valedictorian, sharing the values he instilled in me, and I'd dedicate my speech to him. And there would be many more experiences to share—my college years, my first "real job," my wedding, his grandchildren. We would be closer than he and his father had been. For him, this would be his most fulfilling achievement as a parent.

Sadly, this was not to be. If only he'd pretended he hadn't heard the knock, you know how you do when someone is selling something you don't want. If only he hadn't opened the door and unknowingly let cancer in. We would have had a lifetime together instead of just 1,313 days.

Perhaps I'll write another "What Might Have Been" sometime down the road as a blog post or journal entry. Once again, it will be written from Mark's voice and will list all the things he'll miss out on, the events and milestones that often come naturally if we live to some ripe old age. The list might look like this:

- The first birthday I missed was my twenty-first, and there are many more uncelebrated ones to come.

- I will never graduate from college, enter the workforce, earn a paycheck, or invest in a 401(k).
- I will never own my own home or experience the smell of a brand new car.
- I can no longer donate my time to causes close to my heart, especially those involving children.
- I won't rack up frequent-flier miles or add stamps to my passport as I travel to new and exotic places.
- I won't slam beers with friends at happy hour or enjoy intimate dinners with a mate.
- I will never be a husband, father, or grandfather.
- I will never grow old in the human sense.
- I am forever twenty.

As for me, I remain a living, breathing, feeling, thinking human. My little family has been fractured, leaving me to carry on. And carry on is what I will do, not only for myself but in honor of Alan and Mark.

chapter 18
We Three

*I am learning to trust the journey, even
when I do not understand it.*

—Mila Bron

Early one morning, just days after Mark's passing, I was lying in bed in a semiconscious state. I was awake enough to realize I was about to begin yet another day without Mark's presence. My new normal feelings of dread, sadness, and grief surfaced, where they sat like a lead vest on my chest. As I lay there with my eyes closed, aware of the quiet and semidarkness of the room, I heard Mark speak three words in a distant, almost whisper-like voice: "I am home."

During my first session with Thomas, the medium, he made it clear Mark had completed his earthly mission. His exact words were, "Mark did not die. He moved. He went into the light." Those three words spoken by Mark, the only time I've heard his sweet, familiar voice since his passing, reinforce for me the possibility there exists some sort of theme in the number three and how it relates to the human experiences of Alan, Joan, and Mark.

I did some research on the meaning and significance of this reoccurring digit and learned that three is considered the number of the divine and is regarded as sacred in many religions. For example, in the Bible, the number three is shown to represent wholeness, completeness, and perfection. The number three is also the number of time:

- Past, Present, Future
- Birth, Life, Death
- Beginning, Middle, End

In regard to my triad, I think Confucius best sums up the meaning of our shared journey: "Three people are walking together; at least one of them is good enough to be my teacher."

I've known for quite some time that Mark wasn't "mine." He was my human child, but I was never in charge of his journey. I provided him with food, shelter, clothing, and guidance as he morphed from infant to toddler to teenager to young adult. I attempted to teach him right from wrong and to instill in him a sense of purpose and community. And that's where my lessons and ability to influence his journey ended. Alan, Mark, and I made a pact to come to this lifetime as a unit. The three lead characters in this earthly drama played out their roles as written in the script of their creation. And when that script called for not one but two tragic scenes, Alan and Mark fulfilled their part and made their exit, leaving me here to fulfill mine.

I came across a quote several years ago from an unknown author I believe best summarizes our earthly relationships and encounters: "God doesn't give you the people you want; He gives you the people you need…to help you, to hurt you, to leave you, to love you, to make you into the person you were meant to be."

I've met and interacted with countless individuals in my time here on Earth, and not a single encounter was initiated via chance or luck. As the tenets of the religion of joan suggest, everything happens for a reason, and we are here as both student and teacher. Every person we cross paths with is fulfilling their part in a divinely created meeting, which was carefully orchestrated so we can influence and impact each other's journeys. In my opinion, there's simply no disputing the fact Alan and Mark have had the most profound effect on my journey. They were less my students and more my teachers. Neither of them needed copious amounts of time to complete their own earthly lessons and teachings.

I'd be remiss in not sharing a bit about my feelings of deep despair and sadness that resulted first from Alan's passing and then later from the tragic chain of events that resulted in Mark's transition. There have been many moments in my life where I wished my time here was up. With that said, I've never seriously considered taking my own life. If anything, I merely wished I would fade away, putting an end to the challenges and pain that have defined so much of my time here. I generally dismiss these thoughts almost as quickly as they appear because in my gut I know I must see this lifetime through to its predetermined final moment as a means of fulfilling its karmic purpose. It's extremely possible if I were to exit stage left before my final curtain call, I'd have to repeat at least some of my earthly lessons.

In my third session with the medium, I specifically asked, "If I were to take my own life, would I have to repeat the lessons of this lifetime?" Before I could actually get that sentence out of my mouth, he replied with an emphatic "Yes." According to Thomas, on my next incarnation, I'd definitely have to relive and repeat all the pain, loss, and suffering I've experienced in this lifetime. Oh my! The mere thought of facing a do-over of certain lessons I've already completed and lived through is extremely unappealing and rather disturbing. It seems obvious we aren't meant to fully understand the why of our human existence. We must trust and have faith in the process, and one day when it's our time to cross over, our many questions will be answered.

I continue to walk my journey of grief and will do so for some unspecified amount of time. I will use my spiritual beliefs as my walking stick or guide as I meander on this rocky, winding, unfamiliar terrain. I will rely on the ladies of the club and a few other trusted friends for support and social engagements as well as for a safe place to cry, vent, and rationalize my sometimes irrational thoughts and feelings. I will schedule appointments with Thomas as needed and seek other methods of connecting with spirit, which includes time spent daily in meditation. I'm determined to learn to quiet my mind, one that seems to have no off switch. I will use my journal and blog as places to express myself as well as a method to continue honing my writing skills. Like meditation, I think the key lies in practice, practice, practice. I will continue to drink from the reservoir of resilience, the sweet elixir that nurtures and nourishes our innate gift of inner strength. And lastly, I will spend time in nature, which also provides food for the soul. Speaking of food, we recently hung two bird feeders in our backyard, as it seemed only fitting I should give back to the creatures who've given so much to me. Their delicate beauty, inspiration, and song as well as their connection to another realm have contributed to my quest for peace and acceptance.

As I've shared, I know for a fact that Mark's spirit lives on. I believe he often stood beside me as I wrote, perhaps even placing words into my head where they could find their way out through my fingers. Also, I included Mark's writings as a way to share his profound insights and wisdom. I believe his words should be considered as sage advice from an old soul. My son's most recent incarnation as Mark Johann Hyams was full of purpose and meaning, and I know he impacted others in a positive way. I also know he lived his life in honor of his father and the goals Alan had for young Mark as he grew into a man. In Mark's baby book, there's a page for "Dad's Thoughts." In response to the question "My wishes for you," Alan wrote the following: "Learn to be compassionate and giving."

I choose to believe Mark's life will be honored, remembered, and reflected upon by many for some time to come. It is my goal and mission to ensure he's never forgotten, and I have proof I'm already fulfilling this commitment. During my third session with the medium, he informed me I keep Mark very much alive here on Earth. For an instant, I considered that perhaps this was a bad thing. Maybe I was keeping Mark from his own divine pursuits? This thought was swiftly dismissed by Thomas with these words:

"Keeping Mark alive here on Earth is a good thing."

After

Goodbyes are only for those who love with their eyes. Because for those who love with heart and soul, there is no such thing as separation.

—Rumi

Not long ago, I stepped onto the deck and took some time to stand in the quiet among the nature that exists outside our back door. It was wintertime, so most of the trees were naked, having shed their coats of leaves as the days had grown shorter and the temperatures plummeted. Only the peace-loving pine trees retained their cloaks of green, providing some color to an otherwise gloomy, brown, and barren landscape. I glanced up at one towering evergreen in the hope of catching a glimpse of the large nest that had been home to a mother hawk and her sole offspring. The two of them had provided me with feelings of wonder and awe as I witnessed the inner workings of their life as mother and child. I've been told by a hawk expert that a mother hawk will often return to the same nest year after year as she continues to add to her family. As I peered into the spaces between branches, it became obvious the nest was gone. What had happened? I searched the yard and brush line, expecting to find the remnants of this one-time home, but no visible evidence had been left behind. Perhaps the nest was too weak and fragile to withstand the whipping, frigid winds that frequently blow our way this time of year.

So it seems possible Momma Hawk won't be nesting within the confines of my backyard as the seasons shift once again, depriving me of my role as spectator to her life. Mark's physical presence will also be absent this spring just as it's been for far too many days and nights. He has flown the coop, and just like Momma Hawk and her child, it was time for him to go, to move on. I share this quote by Mark Slouka: "Gone—the saddest word in any language."

I loved that boy with every ounce of my being and will continue to love him forever. I take comfort in the fact he didn't "die," and I believe without question we will be together again one day. And when the time comes for me to shed my earth suit and cross over, Alan and Mark will be there to guide me home.

I leave you with a quote from Buddha I believe sums up this thing called life. It also happens to reiterate and reinforce this tale of three—the story of Alan, Joan, and Mark.

"In the end, only three things matter: how much you loved, how gently you lived, and how gracefully you let go of things not meant for you."

Alan and Joan's Wedding
Cincinnati, Ohio, July 9, 1995

Alan and Mark at the Hospital
Houston, Texas, February 13, 1998

Alan, Joan, Mark, and Fritz—Fritz's Birthday Party
Houston, Texas, July 2, 2000

Alan and Mark in Our Front Yard
Houston, Texas, Spring 2000

Mark and Joan, Mom Prom
Cincinnati, Ohio, February 6, 2016

Mark Hyams, Senior Picture
Cincinnati, Ohio, October 23, 2015

Bibliography

Brown, Brenè. *The Gifts of Imperfection—Let Go of Who You Think You're Supposed to Be and Embrace Who You Are.* New York: Simon & Schuster, 2010.

Cain, Susan. *Quiet: The Power of Introverts in a World That Can't Stop Talking.* New York: Crown Publishing Group, 2012.

Callanan, Maggie, and Patricia Kelley. *Final Gifts: Understanding the Special Awareness, Needs, and Communications of the Dying.* New York: Bantam Books, 1992.

Connor, Kathryn M. "Assessment of Resilience in the Aftermath of Trauma," *The Journal of Clinical Psychiatry* 67 suppl. 2 (2006) 46-49.

Dickinson, Emily. "Hope is the thing with feathers."

Downey, Allen "The retreat from religion is accelerating" *Probably Overthinking It* October 20, 2017 http://allendowney.blogspot.com/2017/10/the-retreat-from-religion-is.html

Kurcinka, Mary Sheedy. *Raising Your Spirited Child: A Guide for Parents Whose Child Is More Intense, Sensitive, Perceptive, and Energetic.* New York: HarperCollins Publishers, 1991.

Joan's Library

The tenets of the religion of joan were largely downloaded into my brain via reading. Lots. Of. Reading. I credit *Embraced by the Light* as my first spiritual book. I read it not long after the passing of my father in 1996, and since then I've read and continue to read books that are spiritual in nature. Below is a partial list of the books that both awakened and inspired me as well as a few individuals, magazines, and songs that also influenced my spiritual enlightenment.

Books

Allenbaugh, Kay. *Chocolate for the Woman's Soul.*
Bodine, Echo. *Echoes of the Soul—The Soul's Journey Beyond the Light Through Life, Death and Life After Death.*

Callanan, Maggie and Patricia Kelly. *Final Gifts— Understanding the Special Awareness, Needs and Communications of the Dying.*

Carlson, Richard and Benjamin Shield. *Handbook for the Soul.*

Chodron, Pema. *Start Where You Are—A Guide to Compassionate Living.*

Eadie, Betty J. *Embraced by the Light.*

Frankl, Viktor E. *Man's Search for Meaning.*

Hanh, Thich Nhat. *Anger—Wisdom for Cooling the Flames.*

Hay, Louise L. *You Can Heal Your Life.*

Hay, Louise L. *Heal Your Body.*

Kabat-Zinn, Jon. *Wherever You Go There You Are— Mindfulness Meditation in Everyday Life.*

Kagan, Annie. *The Afterlife of Billy Fingers—How My Bad-Boy Brother Proved to Me There's Life After Death.*

MacLaine, Shirley. *The Camino—A Journey of the Spirit.*

Moorjani, Anita. *Dying To Be Me: My Journey From Cancer to Near Death, To True Healing.*

Myss, Caroline. *Sacred Contracts.*

Myss, Caroline. *Anatomy of the Spirit.*

Pausch, Randy. *The Last Lecture.*

Roman, Sanaya. *Spiritual Growth—Being Your Higher Self.*

Shapiro, Debbie. *The Bodymind Workbook.*

Tolle, Eckhart. *The Power of Now.*

Van Praagh, James. *Reaching to Heaven—A Spiritual Journey Through Life and Death.*

Vanzant, Iyanla. *Faith in the Valley—Lessons for Women on the Journey to Peace.*

Walsch, Neale Donald. *Conversations with God: Books 1, 2 & 3*.
Walsch, Neale Donald. *The New Revelations—A Conversation with God*.
Walsch, Neale Donald. *Tomorrow's God*.
Williamson, Marianne. *The Gift of Change—Spiritual Guidance for a Radically New Life*.
Williamson, Marianne. *Return to Life—Reflections on the Principles of A Course in Miracles*.
Zukav, Gary. *The Seat of the Soul*.

Magazines

The Sun
Unity

Authors/Speakers

Deepak Chopra, MD
Wayne Dyer, PhD
Andrew Weil, MD

Songs

"Dancing in the Sky" by Dani & Lizzy Nelson
"Imagine," performed by John Lennon and cowritten with Yoko Ono
"What a Wonderful World," performed by Louis Armstrong (written by George Weiss and Robert Thiele)

Acknowledgements

Thank you. Grateful. Humbled. These are the words that best acknowledge and summarize the appreciation I have for those who have contributed to my life and more recently, the conception and birth of this book.

To my spiritual mentors and kindred spirits, Sandra Montalbano and Susan Marshall, I know our paths crossed for a reason many years ago. And those encounters changed my life forever. You ladies are the "s" in spirit.

A *large* thank you to medium Thomas Windlow for sharing his gift with me. The words you shared from Mark, Alan, and my parents have aided in my healing and solidified the truth that nothing dies.

To the mothers (and fathers and siblings) in the Club, I am grateful to know you, though I wish that what connects us was less tragic and sad. Simply said, I wish we still had our children together with us on this side.

To the countless people—family, friends, neighbors, and strangers—who have thought about and prayed for us in the days, weeks, and months following Mark's passing, I am eternally grateful. I know that like God and a few birds, you, too, have carried us. I'm especially grateful to Therese Fledderjohn for all of her text messages and gifts from the heart. To borrow her words, she "lifts me up." Something each and every one of us should do *and* can do every day.

To the many who donated more than $6,000 to the Juvenile Diabetes Research Foundation (JDRF) in Mark's name, I extend a huge and heartfelt thank you. I'll continue to hope for a cure for type 1 diabetes, and it can't come soon enough.

To my beta readers, Jane Bretl, Dauna Easley, and Nan Hartup, I can never thank you enough for your time and input that enabled me to move this project forward. After four months of solitary writing, I knew I could trust you with my baby.

To my editor, Miranda Miller, your editing skills, tutorials, and positive reinforcement enabled me to raise the quality of my writing and helped me produce a book that can compete with works that are traditionally published. Under your tutelage, I've learned a lot about adverbs, commas, contractions, and my affliction with "that" disease. And it doesn't hurt that you're a fellow Buckeye.

To my parents, Alois and Hildegard Stadler, thank you for my German roots. My DNA coupled with your plow forward life skills instilled in me a work ethic and drive that contributes to my ability to stand in the face of adversity.

To my sister, Betsy Russell, you have gone above and beyond on behalf of my family. Thank you for your help in April 2001 when you took time away from your young children and job to travel to Houston to take care of Alan while I worked. And then two years later when you took Mark into your home while I was hospitalized, not once but twice. You were much more than a sister-in-law and aunt. Alan, Mark, and I are blessed to call you family.

To my current husband, Guy Schmitz, I've already devoted a few paragraphs of a chapter to your endearing qualities, so enough said. I've been pondering the recent revelation that we've spent at least four lifetimes together. It seems possible you were the funnier one in a previous life. I have dibs on this one.

To Alan and Mark, there is no story without you. I hope this book meets with your approval. I wrote it as a means of sharing your story and legacy, one that should be noted for the ages. I thank you for showing up at my sessions with Thomas and for watching over me. I look forward to the time when we will be together again.

To Mark, remember to "sleep tight, and don't let the bedbugs bite."

Author Bio

Joan Hyams Schmitz writes to offer food for thought to anyone willing to read her stories. Much of her material was acquired at the School of Hard Knocks, where she maintains a front-row seat. Life has tossed her more than her fair share of lemons, which resulted in many batches of lemonade. Joan has always been fascinated with the human mind, leading to both a degree in psychology and a lifetime of reading, self-reflection, neuroses dissection, spiritual exploration, and countless hours spent on a counselor's couch. Her hard-won insights and wisdom gained via age, coupled with German genes and the roar of Leo the Lion, have enabled Joan to remain vertical when life has attempted to knock her down. Multiple times. She can be found, sipping from a glass of lemonade, in a home she shares with her husband in a suburb of Cincinnati, Ohio.

You can find Joan via her blog *Joan's Jottings* at jfh48.blog, via email at schmitzjf@outlook.com, on her website www.joanschmitz.com, or on Facebook by typing in *all* of her names: Joan Stadler Hyams Schmitz.

www.ingramcontent.com/pod-product-compliance
Lightning Source LLC
Chambersburg PA
CBHW020413080526
44584CB00014B/1300